Sport, Sectarianism and Society in a Divided Ireland

Sport, Politics and Culture

A series of books from Leicester University Press

Series editors: Stephen Wagg
Department of Sociology, University of Leicester
John Williams
Sir Norman Chester Centre for Football Research,
University of Leicester

Sport, Sectarianism and Society in a Divided Ireland

JOHN SUGDEN AND ALAN BAIRNER

LEICESTER UNIVERSITY PRESS
LEICESTER, LONDON AND NEW YORK

DISTRIBUTED IN THE UNITED STATES AND CANADA BY ST. MARTIN'S PRESS

Leicester University Press
(a division of Pinter Publishers Ltd.)

First published in 1993

Editorial offices
Fielding Johnson Building, University of Leicester,
Leicester LE1 7RH, England

Trade and other enquiries
25 Floral Street, London WC2E 9DS *and*
Room 400, 175 Fifth Avenue, New York, NY 10010, USA

John Sugden and Alan Bairner are hereby identified as the authors of this work as provided under Section 77 of the Copyright, Designs and Patents Act, 1988.

British Library Cataloguing in Publication Data

A CIP catalogue record for this book is available from the British Library

ISBN 0 7185 1457 2

Library of Congress Cataloging-in-Publication Data

Sugden, John Peter.
    Sport, sectarianism, and society in a divided Ireland / John Sugden and Alan Bairner.
        p.   cm. – (Sport, politics, and culture)
    Includes bibliographical references (p.   ) and index.
    ISBN 0–7185–1457–2
    1. Sports – Northern Ireland. 2. Sports – Political aspects – Northern Ireland. 3. Sports – Social aspects – Northern Ireland. 4. Sports – Northern Ireland – Religious aspects – Catholic Church. 5. Sports – Northern Ireland – Religious aspects – Protestants.
    I. Bairner, Alan. II. Title. III. Series.
    GV605.5.S84 1993
    796′.09416–dc20   92–42149
                                                                           CIP

Typeset by Mayhew Typesetting, Rhayader, Powys
Printed and bound in Great Britain by SRP Ltd, Exeter

CONTENTS

ACKNOWLEDGEMENTS

The authors would like to express their gratitude to colleagues and students at the University of Ulster at Jordanstown for their valuable advice and critical reactions to ideas expressed in this book. We would also like to thank Alec McAulay at Leicester University Press for his encouragement and guidance, Stephen Wagg and John Williams for their editorial assistance, and Jane Evans at Leicester University Press for editorial and production work. Both of us are indebted to family and friends for their enthusiasm and forbearance during the preparation of this work. Finally, we would like to thank the many members of the Northern Ireland sporting community who have been a constant source of stimulation and for whom this book is largely written.

INTRODUCTION

In Northern Ireland, all significant aspects of life are bound up with the politics of division. Sport is no exception. Indeed, in a region where sport and politics are both pursued with passion, it is inevitable that the two worlds will collide. Even those people who argue that sport and politics should not mix are forced to admit that in various circumstances the playing of sport can be adversely affected by external political considerations. For many years, teams and individual athletes have avoided coming to Northern Ireland because of fears for security generated by continuing political violence. The Northern Ireland national association football team was obliged to play 'home' fixtures at various English grounds during the early 1970s when other national sides refused to travel to Belfast. In this respect, sport was the innocent victim of civil unrest.

What is less easy for the defenders of the apolitical character of sport to accept is the fact that sport can be an integral element in the creation and exacerbation of political conflict. For instance, on the weekend of 18 and 19 February 1990, Northern Ireland once more captured the headlines of the international news media. The featured item concerned serious rioting which had taken place during and after a football match between Linfield and Donegal Celtic at Windsor Park, Belfast, home of Linfield Football Club and the venue for Northern Ireland's international matches. This incident was much more than just another outbreak of football hooliganism. The character of the two clubs involved and the nature of the support they attract can only be explained with reference to the politics of division. In this case the violence derived from the fact that the conflict between unionism and nationalism in Northern Ireland defines the character of Protestant Linfield and Catholic Donegal Celtic. Politics is integral to their rivalry. Far more than merely offering an example of sport being adversely affected by politics, this match had its own intrinsic political character.

As will be shown, it is this kind of integral linkage between politics and sport which is difficult to avoid in Northern Ireland. Former flyweight world boxing champion, Barry McGuigan, attempted to distance himself from the politics of the area by entering the ring under the banner of the United Nations rather than alienate one or other section of the community. But this gesture failed to overcome the powerful processes of sectarian identification which operate in the Province and which make it almost impossible for anyone to avoid being labelled. In McGuigan's case, because, albeit for sporting reasons, he had chosen to pursue his boxing career in the United Kingdom and Northern Ireland rather than in his native Irish Republic, it was possible for nationalists to claim that he was a traitor and refer to him scornfully as 'Barry the Brit'.

There are many more examples like this and it is surprising that, apart from a small number of tentative observations (Sugden and Bairner, 1986; Holt, 1989), Northern Ireland has been largely ignored as a venue for the investigation of the relationship between sport and politics. Few political problems in modern times have attracted as much academic and journalistic attention as the conflict in Northern Ireland. Since the late 1960s the eyes of the world have been focused at regular intervals on a small region, geographically located in the north-east corner of the island of Ireland and constitutionally part of the United Kingdom. The civil unrest and the various political and security responses, which collectively have become known as the Troubles, are the consequence of a political 'settlement' reached in the 1920s which brought about the partition of Ireland. This involved on the one hand, the creation of the Irish Free State (later the Republic of Ireland) and on the other, in response to the resistance of those who supported the continued Union of Great Britain and Ireland (Unionists), the establishment of a devolved Northern Ireland government, politically tied to Westminster and presiding over six of the nine counties of the historic Province of Ulster.

The population of this new political entity consisted of approximately two-thirds whose heritage and Protestant religious persuasion inclined them towards Unionism and one-third who were indigenously Irish and Catholic. This demographic imbalance created an in-built political majority for Unionists in the Stormont Parliament which they used to consolidate their ascendancy at the expense of the Catholic minority through discrimination in such areas as housing, employment and electoral practice. In the mid-1960s, civil rights activists began to draw attention to the iniquities of the prevailing system and to demand fairer treatment for Catholics in Northern Ireland. Initially this did not involve serious questioning of the constitutional position. The refusal by many leading Unionist politicians to give any ground and the violent response to civil rights demonstrations by members of the security forces, particularly the locally recruited and almost exclusively Protestant 'B' Special Constabulary, created the conditions which broadened the basis for conflict. Principally, this involved the introduction of the British Army to deal with problems of public disorder in the streets of Belfast and Londonderry. Partly as a result, the issue of civil rights became subsumed by a more traditional Irish nationalist campaign for the independence of the whole of Ireland, heralding the re-emergence of the Irish Republican Army (I.R.A.) as a potent paramilitary force in the Province.

After more than 20 years of the Troubles, Northern Ireland is a society deeply divided along sectarian lines. The specific contours of the Troubles may have changed over the years, but the essential problem of two separate communities with different traditions and holding distinctive aspirations remains intractable. A wide variety of political strategies has been suggested and several have been implemented without any conspicuous success. It seems that tribal loyalties are impervious to such initiatives. Nevertheless, the bulk of academic research on Northern Ireland tends to focus on the institutional constituents of the conflict, examining in great detail the governmental process, the character of political parties, local government, the international dimension and the like. With the exception of studies of the role of the main churches in Northern Ireland, little attention has been paid to those elements of civil society which define the very existence of the two communities, even though the oppositional solidarity of Nationalists and Unionists, although largely defined by religious affiliation, is cemented by exposure to a related range of cultural activities and ideological beliefs.

Other than the church, probably the most important sources of community divisiveness are educational background, neighbourhood affiliation and sports preference. While the importance of education and community segmentation has been recognised, the complex role which sport plays in civil and political relations in the Province has been largely neglected. This is surprising since there is a high level of attention paid to sport in Ireland in general and in Northern Ireland in particular, in terms of participation, spectatorship and armchair interest. With a population of less than 1.5 million Northern Ireland has produced a disproportionate number of top-class performers in athletics, rugby, association football, field hockey, motor sports, snooker, boxing, equestrianism, and Gaelic games. The passion with which the people of this troubled society pursue their sports could be interpreted as a form of escapism into a world which is in some way far removed from the social and political travails of everyday living. Indeed, sports administrators, politicians and some journalists would claim that sport and leisure provide a neutral domain for the amelioration of damaged community relations. However, as the Linfield/Donegal Celtic incident revealed in the most dramatic fashion, sport is by no means immune from the sectarian undercurrents which sustain Northern Ireland's political impasse. In fact, incidents of this sort are more than passive reflections of political divisions. By its very nature, sport provides a focus for sectarian identification and a forum for confrontation which, in tandem, exacerbate conflict. In addition, state-sponsored attempts to use forms of sport and recreation to defuse the volatile situation seriously underestimate the important strategic significance of these areas of popular culture in defining the boundaries between the two warring factions.

This book is the first major examination of the multifaceted political nature of sport and leisure in Northern Ireland. It is the product of a number of years of experience of and research into sport, leisure and socio-political relations in the Province. It is impossible to live, work and play in Northern Ireland without realising that sport and politics are intertwined. Neither of the authors is a native of Northern Ireland, but both have lived, worked and played there for over 10 years. Their professional academic interests in politics and sociology in combination with an enthusiasm for sport provided the impetus for this work. What follows is an attempt to make sense of the various ways in which sport is dialectically linked with social attitudes and political practices. It is intended that the book should fulfil three overlapping functions. First, it is a book about the political sociology of sport in Northern Ireland. However, because it is impossible to make sense of the socio-cultural characteristics of sport in the Province without gaining insight into the salient features of the wider political crisis, it is, secondly, an addition to the literature concerned with the political sociology of Northern Ireland in general. Finally, through analysing sport, leisure and political division in Northern Ireland, the book contributes to the growing body of knowledge about sport and politics in general.

In the opening chapter we outline the general theoretical context within which our analysis of sport in Northern Ireland is contained. This involves investigating the confrontational nature of sport in the modern world and exploring those sociological principles which help us to understand how sport has become the focus for political exploitation. We also present a summary of our position on the role of sport in the articulation of power in society. This necessitates an explanation of the relationship between the state in Northern Ireland and the forces which do most to determine the shape and substance of the Province's distinctive civil societies – namely, sectarianism, ethnicity, nationalism and social class.

In Chapter 2 the most overtly political sporting body, the Gaelic

Athletic Association (G.A.A.) is scrutinised. There is an historical account of the development of the Association which was established with the expressed intention of resisting the spread of what were regarded by Irish nationalists as the foreign, English sports of cricket and rugby. The revival of Gaelic games was viewed as part of the wider struggle for national identity. Particular attention is paid to two important periods in the history of the G.A.A.: the formative years in the volatile period leading up to the partition of Ireland and the Civil War in the early 1920s; and the contemporary position of the organisation committed to the ideal of a 32-county, independent Irish state, but obliged to conduct its affairs in two separate political entities. The symbolic phenomenon of openly Irish sports being played in that part of Ireland which has resisted the call for national unification provides important insights into the deeply rooted character of ethnic and cultural differences in Northern Ireland.

Chapter 3 examines the role of sports which are designated as English and foreign by Irish nationalists and supporters of Gaelic games. The three sports analysed are hockey, cricket and, in even greater detail, rugby union. The origins and early development of anglophile sports are traced to highlight the extent to which their presence in Ireland is the direct result of British influence. This chapter assesses the current position of these sports as they are played in Northern Ireland and the subculture which surrounds them. Despite the fact that the three sports can be played at international level by teams chosen from throughout Ireland and regardless of the well-established contacts between players from both parts of the island, it is argued that within Northern Ireland itself the origins of these sports are still reflected in the character of the people and the communities which support them. Furthermore, the subtleties of Irish political divisions, which are part of the fabric of Irish hockey and rugby, occasionally rise to the surface in episodes described in the chapter. It is shown that although the anglophile sports perform a function in bringing together citizens of the Irish Republic and Northern Ireland, in the latter they remain the almost exclusive preserve of Unionists. As such, their integrative potential is severely limited.

This is followed by a chapter which focuses on sports which have a global appeal. Particular attention is paid to association football as the world's most popular game. Once again, attention is paid to the early development of soccer in Ireland, but for the most part, this section deals with the period since partition. It explores relations between the Irish Football Association (I.F.A.), which administers the game in Northern Ireland, and the Football Association of Ireland (F.A.I.), which is the governing body in the Irish Republic. The attitudes of the people in Northern Ireland to the existence of two separate Irish international sides are examined. Football is a universal game and wherever it is played in the world it is appropriated as a forum for the expression of ethnocentric and nationalistic rivalries. In this respect Northern Ireland is unexceptional. The chapter provides a detailed account of the relationship between sectarian politics and football in the Province. Despite its universality, which means that it cannot be characterised as belonging to one or other community in Northern Ireland, football is chauvinistically appropriated by both Catholics and Protestants making it more divisive than reconciliatory.

While Chapters 2, 3 and 4 are informed by an understanding of politics in its widest, cultural sense and focus exclusively on the most visible aspects of sport in Northern Ireland, Chapters 5 and 6 look at the institutional structure of sport, leisure and recreation provision and the political apparatus through which such provision is sustained. As the main brokers of central government policy and funding for sport and leisure, the Department of Education for Northern Ireland (D.E.N.I.) is scrutinised. Special attention is paid to the educational system, the Sports Council for Northern Ireland, the extensive local government involvement in leisure and the sport and leisure dimensions of a variety of government-sponsored community relations initiatives.

The conclusion revisits the issues raised in the opening chapter and develops them in the light of the analysis of sport and politics in Northern Ireland. There are two major strands to this concluding investigation. The first highlights the affinity between sport and forms of nationalism and ethnocentrism. The second analyses sport as a realm of civil society which is contested at every level of political activity, including that of the state. On this basis an attempt is made to weave together the rudiments of a theory of sport and politics which not only accounts for the situation in Northern Ireland, but which has the potential for universal application.

1

SPORT, POLITICS AND POWER RELATIONS

In this book we argue strongly that in Northern Ireland sport and politics are intimately bound up with one another and that this locally observed relationship tends to be a feature of sport in the modern world. However, we are not suggesting that sports are inherently political. Rather, we take the position that sports have certain intrinsic qualities which render them particularly susceptible to political manipulation. We also propose that, because of the role it fulfils in the socialisation process, sport has developed as a significant medium, or collection of symbols, through which the individual can identify with a particular social formation, thus exaggerating sport's capacity to become politicised. Thus, we suggest, this is why the modern state, in Northern Ireland and in other advanced societies, seeks to exert a degree of influence over this sphere of civil society. In this chapter we outline some of the important features of our theory of sport, politics and power as it relates to our analysis of Northern Ireland.

THE CONFRONTATIONAL NATURE OF MODERN SPORT

Sports are competitive physical activities through which individuals or groups struggle against each other, either directly or indirectly, for victory. The process through which supremacy is fought for (playing the game) is significant, but the final outcome is decisively important (winning, or not losing). In the face of a distorted overemphasis on winning, there have been experiments to promote participation in non-competitive physical activities, some of which have been stylised as sports. However, unless participants have a goal in mind, albeit an abstract one such as doing better than the last time, it is hard to categorise activities such as jogging or throwing a frisbee as sports. Certainly, non-competitive physical activities do not hold the attention of children and young people for long. Movement for its own sake can have tremendous aesthetic appeal both for participant and onlooker, but it is the competitive quest for excellence that represents the essence of sporting activity. For instance, attempts by the Chinese communists to remove the competitive element in sport failed miserably because, despite the pressure of ideological inducements, participants themselves recognised that attempting to win was essential to the enjoyment of sport. Likewise, while the freely flighted frisbee was adopted as a symbol for the non-competitive games movement in the United States in the 1960s and 1970s, since then Ultimate Frisbee has emerged as a highly popular team game based on the competition for territory which is a feature of the ultra-competitive American ('gridiron') Football.

Whether we like it or not, the most popular sports have always been those which involve humans in direct confrontation with their fellows, particularly team sports which demand a high degree of physical prowess and physical contact. This is not to suggest that as a species we are innately and limitlessly competitive. As Elias and Dunning (1986) argue, there are strong 'civilizing' conventions which attempt to limit the extent to which sporting confrontations lead to aggression within the confines of the activity and which try to prevent an overspill of aggression into the wider community. In this regard, sport can be viewed as both a cathartic release from the routines and bureaucratic form of modern living and a forum for demonstrating restraint and self-control. But sport does not exist in isolation from the rest of society and where there exist powerful cultural forces and stereotypes which identify contestants and fans as enemies outside of the game, evidence suggests that participation in confrontational sports can lead to the augmentation of feelings of militancy among participants and spectators alike before, during and after the sporting contest. The following chapters are full of examples of sporting events in Northern Ireland which have doubled as occasions for sectarian confrontation both on and off the field of play.

This is not to suggest that in and of themselves competitive sports promote social divisions. Within a relatively homogeneous social and cultural context and free from the excessive penetration of extrinsic motivations for victory, sports can help to cement existing solidarity. For instance, despite the endemic problem of football hooliganism in England, one of the most fiercely contested league fixtures, the Merseyside derby between Everton and Liverpool, takes place year after year without significant crowd violence. When either team plays Manchester or London rivals, however, trouble generally ensues. This can only be explained in terms of the high degree of social integration and the strength of shared regional identification on Merseyside which discourages violence between rival Everton and Liverpool fans, but which facilitates aggressive postures towards supporters of teams from other regions. Likewise, when sports participants are taken out of their native cultural settings for extended periods and are allowed to mingle socially with opponents in identical circumstances, political differences can be easily forgotten by individual athletes as bonds are formed through sharing the experience of competition. The fraternal atmosphere of the residential villages at international competitions such as the Olympic and Commonwealth Games exemplifies this. Furthermore, as we discuss in Chapter 5, even against a background of deep-seated social conflict, such as prevails in Northern Ireland, it may be possible that sports can be manipulated to promote better community relations. Nevertheless, the experiences of international athletes are minority ones. For the vast majority of people involved in sport in Northern Ireland and elsewhere, participation and partisanship take place firmly in local cultural settings and reflect the ideologies and prejudices prevailing therein.

The confrontational nature of sports, to some extent, determines and is exaggerated through a structure of organised competition which is progressively territorial, involving individual, local, regional, cultural and national boundaries and pitting neighbour against neighbour, school against school, community against community, town against town, province against province, nation against nation, first world against third world, and, at least through the eyes of the media and sports entertainment industry, black against white and communist against capitalist. At each level of competition, relatively fewer people are directly involved as participants and more people are drawn in as administrators, promoters and supporters. In this way, as the locus of control for defining the context and limits of competition moves progressively away from the athlete towards interests operating outside of the sport, the potential for political and economic interference is increased. There can be little doubt that the vast majority of those who play high-level sport for and/or in Northern Ireland do not consider themselves to be political actors. Nevertheless, the context of their performances and the motivations of those who control and support them have often led to political interference.

THE POLITICAL SOCIOLOGY OF SPORT

None of the above would make complete sense if sport was not such an important bridge between the individual and society. Thus, the real link between sport and politics is a sociological one. The problem of sport acting as a catalyst for political conflict is bound up with the role it has come to play in the process of individual socialisation and community construction. As John Hoberman (1984) has observed, sport has no intrinsic value structure, but it is a ready and flexible vehicle through which ideological associations can be reinforced. As a consequence of child's play, sport is rooted in the earliest experiences of infancy. Later, through a continuum of influences, involving families, peer groups, neighbourhood organisations, schools and the media, sport develops as an important structure of socialisation through which the growing child absorbs lessons in general social values and normative behaviour as she or he plays and watches games. The shared emotions which are generated in the heat of competition become attached to the value structure within which the sport is played. From an early stage in our lives we are taught and learn to make the connection between the playing of the game and the ideals which the game has come to stand for. The older we get and the more competent we become the less we are allowed to play the game for its own sake or watch our representatives in an ideological vacuum. For school, for family, for God, for money, for monarch and for country gradually displace fun as the forms of rationale for taking part in sports and taking sides as spectators.

While most never become top-class athletes, the vast majority of us are made intimately familiar with the first stages of the nursery systems of most major sports and this familiarity is developed into high-level national and international competition through the efforts of the media. Thus, we become sports fans with a strong vicarious and emotional attachment to the top-class performers who are selected to represent our way of life in competition on the national and international circuit and who are burdened with our generalised sense of collective pride. This connection is clearly exaggerated through the hype and jingoistic trimmings which surround modern sports. It is estimated that the 1990 World Cup in Italy was seen on television at some stage by more than half of the world's population. No doubt each national audience was subjected to a torrent of chauvinistic interpretations, none of which could have furthered the cause of internationalism. However, even without hysterical commentators, flag ceremonies and medal counts, the average sports fan by early adulthood is sufficiently steeped in local and national sports creeds to have a strong surrogate identification with elite sports performers and, as they win or lose, it is through the ethnocentric abstraction of 'our side', with all of its ideological baggage, that we register and internalise victory or defeat.

Thus, despite the idealism of certain sports practitioners and administrators, who cling to the cherished belief that sport is or should be free from politics, historical evidence reveals that this is rarely the case. Indeed the greatest showcase of international sport, the Olympic

Games, has been consistently enveloped by political controversy and intrigue. Successive boycotts, political protests by competitors, terrorist attacks and political squabbling among the members of the International Olympic Committee (I.O.C.) have all contributed to the increased politicisation of the Olympic movement. However, the modern Olympics have always had their own political dimension, rooted in the competition for national prestige which inspired their reincarnation at the end of the nineteenth century. Moreover, this relationship is manifest in a whole range of sporting activities and is by no means limited to the Olympic Games. Indeed, the close relationship between sport, as an aspect of popular culture, and national identity has always rendered it vulnerable to political exploitation.

In modern history the connection between organised sport and nationalism is undoubtedly largely a product of British imperialist expansion, through which political and economic subjugation was supplemented by cultural and ideological forces, among which sports and recreation were central features. Elsewhere the political potential of sport was exploited by the Fascist regimes of Mussolini and Hitler which developed the strategy of promoting national and racial supremacy through physical culture. Simultaneously, after the Russian revolution, the Soviet leaders came to use sport as a means of forging a sense of national and political unity. Sports policy was determined wholly by the Communist Party. After the Second World War, with the emergence of many client communist states such as East Germany, Czechoslovakia, Poland and, later, Cuba, all of which endorsed the demonstration of political and economic achievement through sporting prowess, the confrontational nature of international sports was emphasised in the atmosphere of the Cold War.

At one level, this means that the intense political and military rivalry between the United States and the Soviet Union in the 1950s and 1960s was translated into a competition for sporting supremacy. Other members of the rival power blocs played their part in the politicisation of sport, first by taking part in the communist versus capitalist medal count, and secondly, by asserting their separate national identities when in competition with one another. The latter had been particularly evident prior to 1989 within the Warsaw Pact with smaller states such as Hungary and Czechoslovakia at times finding sport to be the only means of asserting a sense of national independence in their dealings with the Soviet Union. Indeed, as the Soviet Union's influence began to wane, it became clear that sport had been a critical factor in the maintenance of local, regional and national identities.

The use of sport in the politics of division is not exclusive to international relations. The cultural characteristics of a given country's sports structure are usually indicators of the principles of social stratification which govern the relative standing of ethnic, racial and class fractions. South Africa has been the outstanding example of a country which has consciously and constitutionally used sports as a means of consolidating the supremacy of one racial and ethnic group over others. This resulted in a long-running international furore which saw South Africa virtually isolated in world sport. Not only in South Africa is the link between sport and social division apparent, but also in liberal democratic countries the nature of social stratification can be revealed through an examination of who's who and who does what in the world of sports. This may not be the result of overt government policy. Nevertheless, governments are aware of the role which sports can play both in the politics of consent and the maintenance of public order, and of their potential to serve as a focus for inter-community strife or harmony.

With regard to the latter, the state's involvement in sport necessarily enhances its political profile. In socialist countries, hitherto, the administrative apparatus of sport has been clearly located within the state and, as outlined above, this has led to sport having a well-defined political dimension. The picture is less clear in liberal democratic countries, however, where sport is supposed to be more or less a voluntary activity, even though for the past hundred years, and especially since the 1950s, the state has increasingly sought to project its influence into an aspect of popular culture which is closely related to the politics of social control and social division. This begs certain conceptual and theoretical questions about the nature of the relationship between sport and politics.

That such a relationship exists is no longer seriously questioned in academic circles and there is a growing body of literature which focuses on the interplay between politics and sport in its many manifestations. The objectives of such scholarship are generally twofold: first, to add to our understanding of the subtle and complex ways through which sport has been harnessed to the political process; and, second, to use sport as a critical window through which to explore the broader social and political relationships within which it is framed.

POLITICAL AND CIVIL SOCIETIES IN NORTHERN IRELAND

The theoretical framework which underpins this study is based upon a particular understanding of the relationship between politics and society. According to Robert Dahl, a political system is 'any persistent pattern of human relationships that involves, to a significant extent, control, influence, power or authority' (Dahl, 1976: 3). This broad definition means that many associations and forms of activity which are not normally regarded as political do, in fact, possess political systems. In this sense, it is legitimate to talk of the internal politics of sports teams, clubs, leagues, governing bodies and so forth, as well as identifying as political certain inter-organisational relationships such as those which exist between the Football Association and the Football League in England. The analysis which follows will reveal the extent to which personal ambitions and struggles for power and influence at this level are important to the culture of sport and leisure in Northern Ireland. Most definitions of politics, however, are concerned ultimately with activities which are more or less directly related to the activities of the state. As R. N. Berki suggests, 'the politics of the state has been considered vastly more important than any other kind of politics' (Berki, 1977: 1). For some analysts the close relationship between politics and the state has been taken as a justification for concentrating all of their attention on activities which emanate from the central legislative, judicial and executive institutions of a given country. Certainly, this is an important area of political studies and for this reason a substantial section of the book examines the role of the state and state-sponsored initiatives in the development and administration of sport and leisure in Northern Ireland.

To concentrate exclusively on these more formal political themes, however, would enable us to tell just part of the story. The state and its key institutions are not the only vehicles for political activity, just as the administrative politics of a range of voluntary sports bodies are not the only interactions which are concerned with the exercise of power. There is a considerable middle ground in which cultural organisations can be and often are implicated in the articulation of a variety of political positions, the understanding of which requires a more subtle theory of politics. In general, we subscribe to an historical materialist view which indicates that economic relations are central to any understanding of social formations. We recognise, however, that such an approach should not preclude the analysis of non-economic activities such as sport which play a vital role in the articulation and consolidation of power relations. For this reason we have drawn upon the ideas of Antonio Gramsci who makes a distinction between the apparatus of the state, as defined above, and that of civil society which is made up largely of a range of social and cultural institutions which are not usually controlled or coordinated by a centralised government. Nevertheless, Gramsci argues that the support of civil society is necessary for the effective rule of the state and this means that the struggle to secure consent or hegemony is integral to the political process. With this in mind, numerous commentators have adopted Gramsci's concept of hegemony in attempting to explain the political role which sport plays in advanced social formations. This policy, however, is not without its critics.

First, it is argued that Gramscian hegemony theory is necessarily flawed given that the general method upon which it is based – namely Marxism – has been wholly discredited as a result of developments in

Eastern Europe since the 1980s. Second, it is claimed by some critics that, regardless of its point of origin, the hegemony thesis has taken the sociology of sport up a blind alley on account of its inability to deal with sport's 'complex multiplicity of dimensions'. Thus, according to one such critic 'we need to employ a plurality of theoretical perspectives and consequent methods of analysis which are not locked into a pre-set ideological cage' (Haywood, 1986: 238).

A detailed exposition and defence of our use of Gramscian theoretical categories is presented in the final chapter. However, given the above criticisms, several points need to be made at this stage. First, it has never been necessary to adhere slavishly to the principles of orthodox Marxism – whatever they might be – to recognise the analytical value of Gramsci's concept of hegemony. The altered status of Marxism–Leninism as a political ideology, therefore, presents no obstacle to the continued use of hegemony or other Gramscian categories.

As for the direct criticism of the hegemony thesis, it must be admitted that too often it has been applied in such a narrow way as to make it unsuited to exploring the complex role of phenomena like sport in modern society. Specifically, although Gramsci developed the concept of hegemony in order to challenge exclusively economistic interpretations of social and political relationships, many of those who have adopted a Gramscian approach have remained so concerned with the centrality of class in modern social formations that they have failed to appreciate the wider implications of hegemony for other categories of social stratification. In particular, their emphasis on class division has prevented them from understanding that Gramsci's approach is admirably suited to explaining divisions which spring from non-economic sources such as national identity, ethnicity and religion. Such a sin of omission would be unfortunate in the analysis of any society. In the case of Northern Ireland, however, it is a dangerous folly since, although class is by no means a negligible factor in explaining the persistence of political crisis in the Province, any real attempt to explain the problem must come to terms with the character of more potent sources of community conflict. The analysis which follows is based, therefore, on an expanded version of the hegemony thesis which takes into account the existence of two separate civil societies in Northern Ireland and the fact that hegemonic struggle takes place not only between social classes but significantly, and perhaps fundamentally, between communities divided on the basis of ethnicity, national identity and religion, and between each of these communities and the British state.

Thus, the social context of sport in Northern Ireland is bound up in a variety of ways with sectarianism, ethnic and national identification, and social class. Because relationships involving these factors inform much of the following analysis, it is necessary at this stage to spell out what we mean by these concepts, what they mean in relation to each other and how they help to inform our understanding of sport in the region. Because these dimensions of the region's political culture are so closely interwoven, it is difficult to consider them separately and even harder to identify a hierarchy of determination. Nevertheless, before we attempt to explain the relationships between them we shall attempt to summarise what each term means in the context of sport in Northern Ireland.

In its most general sense the term sectarianism is used to describe attitudes, belief systems, symbols and practices through which one group of people sets itself apart from another within an otherwise shared culture. However, the term is usually employed more specifically to describe divisions which are grounded in religious differences. Neither approach adequately covers the situation in Northern Ireland where sectarianism can be best understood in two overlapping ways: first, as a symbolic labelling process through which community divisions are defined and maintained, and second, as an ideological justification for discrimination, community conflict and political violence.

Like anywhere else, being either Catholic or Protestant in Northern Ireland is indicative of holding different perceptions of Christianity. However, unlike in most other places, here these religious labels also symbolise much wider social and political differences. In this way, religion has developed as the most salient feature of two distinctive semiotic systems. The creed a person chooses to follow, or more accurately, the version of Christianity which prevails in the family into which that person is born, signifies his or her membership of one of two distinctive cultural traditions. While there may be a complex interplay of historical factors and contemporary issues which influence the region's political character, it is largely in terms of religious affiliation that the social geography which underpins the Troubles is defined. Sports preference can be seen to stand alongside religious affiliation as an important indicator of a person's cultural and political location. In addition, sports preference can be used to reveal a person's religion and this can be dangerous in a region where religious affiliation not only defines the boundaries of the two cultural traditions, but also identifies many of the targets for cross-community conflict.

This active dimension of sectarianism can be misinterpreted as a theological pathology, that is, people attacking each other over matters of religious interpretation. This is rarely the case in Northern Ireland where sectarian discrimination and sectarian violence take place because religious labels are taken to be synonymous with particular cultural and political preferences. A simple example, based on the experiences of both authors, serves to illustrate this point. The religious persuasion of people who are not indigenous to Northern Ireland is largely taken to be irrelevant to the local population. Being English and Protestant or Scottish and Catholic in Northern Ireland tend not to count in terms of the semiotics outlined above. In these cases religious persuasion is seen to be divorced from affiliation to one or other of the Province's distinctive cultural and political traditions. Thus, it is highly unlikely that either the Englishman or the Scot would be discriminated against or subjected to violence on the grounds of their religious beliefs. It is not possible, however, for people who are from Northern Ireland to abdicate from the wider sectarian implications of their religious heritage and simply being labelled Catholic or Protestant can be sufficient to render a person vulnerable to sectarian abuse. For this reason, short of going to church on Sunday, usually safely within the boundaries of separate communities, few people in the Province go out of their way to advertise their religious affiliation. However, it is not so easy to disguise one's sporting preference, which can be used as an oblique mechanism for determining a person's religious persuasion. Thus, sports participants can be victimised because their chosen sport is placed within a particular cultural tradition and also because their involvement with that sport gives away their religious identity. Finally, because of sport's sectarian symbolism, sporting events are regularly exploited for the expression of sectarian feelings.

Issues involving sectarianism and divided cultural traditions in Northern Ireland are themselves underpinned by deeper questions of ethnicity. The concept of ethnicity is most often used in situations where a region is shared by, and in some cases contested by, two or more communities made distinct from one another through social practices and political preferences which are rooted in different geographical origins, and which become transferred from one generation to the next through time-honoured institutional practices. Ethnicity is not the same as race although these two forms of social division can often overlap, as in the case of South Africa where ethnically distinct groups of Anglo and Dutch Caucasians contest the terrain with ethnically and tribally distinct groups of blacks and Asians. (There is a close conceptual relationship between ethnicity and tribalism, the former being a more developed and more geographically transcendent version of the latter.) Ethnicity has proven to be as potent as race in terms of generating social and political conflict.

In Northern Ireland ethnicity can be usefully employed as an aid to understanding the socio-cultural bedrock which supports the differences between the two communities. An overwhelming majority of Catholics in Ulster are indigenous to the Province with a heritage rooted in Celtic or Gaelic Ireland. In contrast, while most Protestants can legitimately claim to come from families which have been located in Northern Ireland for more than six generations, their origins can be traced back to the migration of lowland Scots and northern English during the sixteenth and seventeenth centuries. Given the absence of any obvious racial distinction between the local population and these migrants, if the latter had arrived on the shores of Antrim without posing a threat to the indigenous population, then there is every chance that by now there would have been a higher level of integration and assimilation than is currently the case. Minor cultural differences may have remained but it is unlikely that these would have featured in any prolonged political conflict.

However, the nature of this migration was that of a plantation: a strategy through which a series of English rulers sought to subjugate the warring Irish of Ulster by forcing whole communities off the land and replacing them, wholesale, with large numbers of Scots and English migrants who, in turn, saw themselves as being in a state of seige (Stewart, 1977). The adoption of local customs and practices was never the intention of these migrants who turned inward to re-create in a foreign land the cultures which had sustained them in their mother countries. The specific struggles surrounding the colonisation of Ireland were part of a more general conflict between European rulers, some of whom held allegiance to Rome and the Catholic Church and others who supported a collection of religious reform movements which constituted Protestantism. Oliver Cromwell was among the latter and it was he who was responsible for much of the plantation of Ulster. Land in the Province was meted out to Cromwell's soldiers, their families and their retainers as rewards for their loyalty and their participation in his various campaigns. Not surprisingly, Protestantism loomed large in the construction of a distinctive community spirit for the planters in Ulster and to this day religion remains as the most important symbol of community division.

Behind this separate religious identity, Ulster's Protestants constructed a whole way of life which as much as possible was independent of and insulated from the activities of the remaining Gaelic population. It is this form of cultural apartheid which is at the root of their distinctive ethnicity and 300 years later, while there are many aspects of the Province's culture which are shared by both traditions, there remain many social practices which are not. Distinctive orientations towards occupation, education, newspapers, music and other forms of entertainment are just some of the more obvious preferences which help to perpetuate community separation. Likewise the development of sport and related forms of recreation in the region has become embroiled within the institutional processes which sustain a form of social division which is often described as tribal but which can be more accurately characterised as ethnic.

Many popular sports in Northern Ireland can be associated with one or other cultural tradition. However, not all of these sports can be termed nationalistic. Nationalism refers to a mobilisation of sentiments of fidelity to an established nation state or the idea of such. While nationalism can be underpinned by ethnicity, as for instance with the case of Serbian nationalism, it can also transcend ethnicity, as is the situation with the displays of nationalism which we often witness among the diversity of groups which make up the United States of America. In the case of Northern Ireland, nationalism is closer to the former than the latter in that it appears as a more formal political expression of the Province's rival ethnic enclaves. That people from Northern Ireland can, if they so chose, hold Irish and British passports simultaneously as citizens of two nation states, is a formal recognition that the region is beset by problems of nationhood. This facility, as we will see, regularly leads to political disputes within and between national and international sporting bodies. In fact, most people from Ulster identify themselves as either Irish or British depending upon which ethnic group they belong to. However, being mostly pragmatists, sportsmen and sportswomen seem generally prepared to step outside of their ethnic identity should this offer an opportunity to enhance their sporting careers.

The situation becomes even more complex when we consider that, as things stand, the Irish nation state, to which nationalists in the north so often pledge fidelity, does not include the six counties of Ulster within which they dwell. In reality, Irish nationalism in Northern Ireland is directed towards the idea of a 32-county united Irish state rather than the existing 26 counties of the Irish Republic. It is in this nationalistic sense that the political dimension of the Gaelic Athletic Association can best be understood. To borrow a concept from John Hoberman (1992), this organisation deliberately engages in 'sportive nationalism' as it consciously exploits Irish games playing as a means of developing and disseminating ideas associated with a united and independent Ireland. This may be distinct from the sportive nationalism generated as a residual consequence of the achievements of the Republic's soccer team on the international stage. Northern Catholics may view the Irish soccer team as an all-Ireland entity, but this is not necessarily the case for fans from the Republic and elsewhere. It is certainly not the case for the majority of northern Protestants who feel they have their own team to support.

Indeed, the national identity of the Province's Protestant population is much more difficult to divine than that of its Irish counterparts. Understanding their orientations towards sports actually helps to clarify the situation. Throughout the United Kingdom (of Great Britain and Northern Ireland) British nationalism is a relatively weak sentiment in comparison with the nationalism felt within the constituent elements of England, Scotland, Wales and Northern Ireland. With the exception of the latter, the nationalisms of the parts of the United Kingdom tend to be expressed more at the level of culture than in the political arena. Often the sharpest expressions of this nationalism are to be found within sport. For instance, soccer fixtures between England and Scotland or rugby matches between Wales and England are occasions for celebrating and confirming national differences. Such encounters have been traditionally symbolic, however, and have made only a limited contribution to the cause of political devolution, although it can be argued that the abandonment of the Home International soccer series denied the regions a regular opportunity to assert their cultural distinctiveness and as such raised questions about the balance of power within the United Kingdom.

The situation with Northern Ireland is somewhat different from that of Scotland and Wales. When all-Ireland sporting entities are involved in competition with the other regions of the United Kingdom the vast majority of people in Ulster will support the Irish, and will do so with particular gusto when the opponents are the English. However, there may be a subtle but significant difference in the perceptions of Catholics (Irish Northern Irish) and Protestants (British Northern Irish) as they cheer on 'the men in green'. In supporting an all-Ireland rugby team, most northern Protestants will be engaging in a form of cultural-nationalism not dissimilar from the symbolic sportive nationalism of the Scots and the Welsh. However, for reasons to be discussed, because the status of Northern Ireland as a country is even more ambiguous than that of Scotland or Wales and because northern Protestants have a lingering suspicion of anything which has an all-Ireland label, their enthusiasm is somewhat tempered. For northern Catholics, even though there can be a value-added political dimension to their support for the national rugby team, related to the ongoing struggle for national self-determination, this is counterbalanced by a reluctance to be seen affiliating with a sport which clearly belongs to an anglophile tradition.

If, as is the case with soccer, Northern Ireland fields its own national team then the situation is likely to be somewhat different. Protestants and Catholics (unless the Republic is in the same competition) may support the local team, albeit with varying degrees of enthusiasm. Some Catholics will define the team as Irish, or at least more Irish than the opposition, and support it accordingly, although, for reasons detailed in Chapter 4, they are likely to do so from a distance. Others, believing there to be an association between Northern Ireland's soccer establishment and Unionism, will side with the opposition. In contrast, for many northern Protestants, the presence of Northern Ireland sports teams on the world stage is an important confirmation of their quasi-independence from Great Britain and their total independence from the Republic of Ireland. In this regard, their support has more of a political edge and one which becomes sharper with the introduction of political initiatives, like the Anglo-Irish Agreement, which introduce a Republic of Ireland voice into the debate over the Province's future.

The position taken by Northern Irish Protestants on the subject of nationalism warrants further explanation. In Northern Ireland, as elsewhere, sporting events are among the very few occasions in the modern world at which people can openly celebrate their sense of national identification. In the case of Northern Irish Unionists, however, there is considerable confusion surrounding the issue of *which* nation precisely inspires this sense of identity. Examining the character of Unionist affiliation, David W. Miller claims that 'it is true that the Protestant community in Ulster does evoke loyalty, but not as a "nation"'. Indeed, Miller argues that 'the central peculiarity of Ulster's political culture is that no community – not Britain, not the United Kingdom, not "Ulster" and certainly not Ireland – has attained for Ulster Protestants all of the characteristics which a nation commonly possesses in the modern world' (Miller, 1978: 4). It could be argued that most Ulster Protestants in fact acquire a sense of identity in terms of what they are not and, above all, they are not Irish, in the more Celtic and Catholic sense of that concept. There are, however, more positive ingredients in their conception of who they are, for as Tom Nairn puts it, 'there are of course two "nationalities", in the sense of two distinct ethnic-cultural communities, in geographical Ireland'. Indeed, 'there are two potential national communities and states'. Nevertheless, as Nairn correctly observes, 'the malignant crux of the whole question arises from the fact that there are *not* two "nations" corresponding to these communities' (Nairn, 1981: 237–8). Instead, there exist two, more or less distinct, civil societies which provide the main focal points for rival expressions of allegiance. The Protestant civil society is overwhelmingly Northern Irish in its character but it involves numerous British features and even some which are shared with the remainder of Ireland. This explains why, in terms of sport, most Ulster Protestants are able to support sides representing Northern Ireland, Great Britain and Ireland so long as none of these sides excludes members of their community. At times of political uncertainty, however, they are more likely to turn specifically to Northern Irish teams and players, and it is at this point that a more normal sense of national or at least quasi-national identification emerges.

In other regions of the United Kingdom and in the Republic of Ireland the most significant determining factor in social stratification is social class. However, because of the more obvious significance of sectarianism, ethnicity and nationalism in Northern Ireland, social class tends to be marginalised. While sharing the view of O'Dowd *et al*, who argue that 'those who concentrate on class division and class struggle abstracted from repression (sectarianism) face a political cul de sac in the contemporary situation' (O'Dowd *et al*, 1980: 21), we argue that social class is still a powerful delineator of popular culture in Northern Ireland. As such, it must feature as an important part of the social context for sport and related activities. However, it is equally important not to consider social class in isolation from the other variables of stratification outlined above, particularly sectarianism.

In Northern Ireland sectarianism is a part of the fabric of social class and vice versa. As we have seen, divisions based on religious labels in Ireland pre-date the development of industrial capitalism. During the seventeenth and eighteenth centuries conflicts between Protestants and Catholics arose largely from the issue of who owned and worked on the land. As industrialism took hold during the nineteenth century, factional disagreements over working the land were gradually displaced by sectarian disputes over who worked in the mills, factories, docks and shipyards. In England at this time the availability of work and working conditions became clearly articulated in the politics of class, giving rise to guilds, craft associations and ultimately the trade union movement. While a similar process occurred in Northern Ireland, the development of working-class consciousness and the emergence of trade unions were cross-cut by sectarianism. There can be little doubt that employers did not do much to discourage the presence of sectarianism in the workplace. On the contrary, it was a useful tool which could be used to keep the rank and file divided and divert their attention from the politics of industrial exploitation. Attempts at organising general strikes in Belfast in 1907, 1911 and 1919 all foundered as workers' solidarity was broken down by cross-community suspicion and sectarian job protectionism.

In recent years, one of the more formidable displays of workers' power in the United Kingdom occurred in Northern Ireland in 1974 when the Protestant workforce under the banner of the Ulster Workers' Council orchestrated a general strike, not to obtain better pay or improved working conditions, but to sabotage the Sunningdale agreement which allowed for power sharing in Northern Ireland and the establishment of a Council of Ireland. In this way sectarianism continues to be one of the underpinning mechanisms of working-class mobilisation in Northern Ireland. It is for this reason that the more extreme expressions of sectarianism tend to occur within and between rival working-class groupings. Working-class sport and working-class recreation are not immune from this. This is why many of the worst sport-related sectarian incidents involve association football which is largely a working-class game played and watched by both communities. It is also why, under the prevailing conditions, it is inconceivable that soccer could follow the example of rugby union and operate on an all-Ireland basis. Similarly, it helps to explain why attempts to improve community relations through providing sports and leisure facilities in inner-city areas are doomed to failure.

It is clear that in Northern Ireland considerable importance is attached to customs, traditions and symbols, many of which are wholly or at least partly outside of the sphere of state influence. This includes many sporting configurations and it is the political impact of this quasi-autonomous area of Northern Ireland's civil society which will form the major component of our analysis. Three chapters are designed to illuminate the main cultural and political divisions in sport in Northern Ireland. These are categorised as: 1) Gaelic sports; 2) Anglophile sports which are rooted in and remain tied to English rather than Irish traditions; and 3) other sports which, regardless of their origins, attract cross-community affiliation. We have chosen the three codes of football played in the Province as the most visible and popular exemplars of these three categories and, where appropriate, have drawn upon supporting evidence from other sports. In the remaining chapters attention shifts from sport as an element of popular culture to an examination of the ways through which provision of and access to sport and leisure are politicised by the direct and indirect interventions of the state. The concluding chapter reassesses the evidence and arguments presented throughout and concludes with a socio-political theory which explains the relationship between sport, nationalism and the state in Northern Ireland.

2

GAELIC GAMES AND IRISH POLITICS

While almost every sport in the world has been successfully contested by the Irish, one of the more unusual facts of Ireland's sporting scene is that its own national sports are contested virtually exclusively by the Irish themselves. Gaelic games are played extensively within Ireland. However, apart from surviving as minority sports in countries with an Irish immigrant tradition, such as England, Australia, the United States and Canada, Gaelic games cannot be described as international sports in the same way that, for instance, soccer and even cricket are global games. This warrants some explanation. Sports and games do not occur outside of the boundaries of society. Rather they are intimately bound up with community structure, culture and ritual. Anthropologists have observed that sports and games are symbolically reflective of whole ways of life and sociologists build upon this observation to argue that sports can be used as critical windows into the systematic workings of a given social order. Standing alongside other indigenous institutions, the people of Ireland developed a series of pastimes which are distinctively Gaelic in nature and which are a ritualistic celebration of that particular culture. In order to understand why and how Gaelic sports continue to thrive at a time when most other ethnocentric pastimes have been overwhelmed by universal trends in sports and games, it is necessary to have an understanding of the transcending socio-political and historical context within which they are played.

Situated at the western limit of Europe and surrounded by hostile seas, Ireland was not an easy target for wholesale conquest. Unlike mainland Britain, Ireland was not colonised by the Romans and, like Scotland behind Antonine's Wall, the country continued as a centre for a distinctively Celtic culture long after the Ancient British were diluted as an island race through the rise, fall and aftermath of the Roman Empire. Celtic culture was the common denominator which bound together an otherwise diverse and warlike collection of tribal kingdoms spread throughout the ancient provinces of Leinster, Munster, Connaught and Ulster. At different times, Vikings and Normans raided Ireland and established footholds around the coasts, but neither were particularly effective as colonists. The only significant external influence on the island during the early middle ages was Christianity, and even that was given a characteristically Irish flavour. Sustained by a common language, a particular version of Christianity and characteristic forms of art and literature, Gaels and their distinctive culture flourished in relative isolation well into the middle ages.

Gaelic games are dominated by three forms: hurling (camogie for women), handball and football. Of these, hurling has the purest Irish pedigree. Hurling is a territorial team game involving running and the throwing and hitting of a hard ball with open-faced wooden clubs called hurleys. Records of hurling matches date back long before Christendom, the earliest being in 1272 BC, and the sport seems to have been a staple part of Irish community life for more than 2,000 years. Even today, while Gaelic football may be the most popular of Irish sports, because hurling suggests an unbroken link with the island's ancient past, it is considered by purists as the definitively Irish game. As such, the hurley stick has come to symbolise Irish nationalism. Less is known about the origins of handball, a court and ball game similar to that of fives, the game played at English public schools. In the same way that the game of road bowls was introduced into Ireland by foreign soldiers, it is highly likely that handball was imported by successive generations of English and French troops during the late middle ages (Frazer, 1990). Handball is an obvious relative of racquet games such as real-tennis, tennis and squash. However, while in other regions these racquet games have largely taken the place of handball-like activities, in Ireland handball continues to coexist with these other court and ball sports and is especially popular in Gaelic circles.

As is the case for most European countries, there is evidence that rough and tumble forms of village football have existed in Ireland for many centuries. Unlike hurling, however, which involved distinctive equipment and a pattern of play which clearly set it apart from other ball games, folk football, known as Cad in Celtic Ireland, appears to have been similar to the village football played in Britain and throughout continental Europe in the middle ages. The game of Cad will be discussed in greater detail in Chapter 3, but, as Eoghan Corry (1989) observes, while the researcher can find many references to hurling in the annals of Irish history, before the nineteenth century the records on football in any form are scant. This indicates that, unlike hurling, football was not a significant element of traditional Irish culture. Nevertheless, today Gaelic football is played and defined in opposition to non-indigenous forms of football (rugby and soccer) as if it were the chosen sport of ancient Hibernia. In order to make sense of this illusion and the institutional structure within which all modern Gaelic games are played, we require an appreciation of the social and political forces which accompanied the colonisation of Ireland by Britain, the subsequent struggles for emancipation during the nineteenth and early twentieth centuries and, most recently, the Troubles in Northern Ireland.

From the fifteenth century onwards, Ireland was increasingly exposed to foreign influence and subject to growing English political interference. In the wake of military campaigns inspired by Elizabeth I, James I and Cromwell, large parts of Ireland were taken over by English and lowland Scottish farmers who brought with them their own cultural preferences, including Protestantism and affiliation to British political institutions. Before this time, Ireland had been subjected to a degree of foreign domination, notably by the Normans. The strength of the existing Irish culture was such that the alien ways of invaders were more or less absorbed into the fabric of Gaelic traditions, rather than replacing them. However, in the later middle ages, the strategy of planting wholesale garrison communities into Ireland, particularly in the north and east, brought with it a cultural revolution through which the folkways of Celtic Ireland were seriously undermined by traditions imported from across the Irish Sea (Stewart, 1977).

Of the four ancient provinces, Ulster was considered by the Norman-English as the most difficult to subdue. It was the most remote and the princes of Ulster and their followers were thought to be the most fearsome warriors. Military victories were expensive to achieve and rapidly reversed. In the face of this, another strategy was initiated whereby the conquered lands of Ulster were carved up among the victors and populated by large numbers of English and Scottish farmers and artisans who were brought in to displace the indigenous population. As is the case with any mass immigration, wherever possible, the newcomers established communities which closely resembled those which they had left in the old country and re-created cultural traditions which were rooted in Britishness rather than Irishness. Significantly, the plantation of Ireland occurred against a backcloth of the Reformation and religious persecution throughout Europe. Most prominent among the cultural traditions which the English and Scots brought with them to Northern Ireland was a strong affiliation to the Protestant faith. Thus, from the outset the struggle for supremacy and national identity in Ulster had a strong cultural dimension, the cutting edge of which was and remains the religious question. However, there were other fronts to the battle for cultural hegemony and the issue of sport was by no means the least significant.

The plantation encouraged the process through which Ireland became progressively tied to Britain, culminating in the Act of Union in 1800. This was not a smooth and even process and opposition to British domination was intense, both politically and culturally. During the first half of the nineteenth century, however, after several centuries of persecution and repression, a distinctively Gaelic culture was all but extinguished by serial famine and the mass exodus which followed. Alongside the repression of religion and language, Gaelic sports and games were among a long list of pastimes which virtually disappeared as aspects of everyday life. As is the pattern for long-term colonial rule, in place of Irish traditions, the British encouraged the adoption of their own social and cultural *mores*, including the introduction of a range of sports and recreational activities which had their origins in English public schools and which were distinctively anglophile in flavour.

This process of pacification did not go unresisted. The mid-point of the nineteenth century saw a revival in Irish political aspirations with the emergence of the Fenian Movement and the formation of the Irish Republican Brotherhood (I.R.B.) and the Land League. The problem facing organisations such as these was the apparent lack of a collective sense of Irish identity around which to reconstruct the political movement for national independence. In order to boost flagging nationalist ambitions, political activists felt it necessary to help to create the cultural preconditions for independence by reviving and popularising an identity which was distinctively Gaelic and separate from that of the British. The Catholic faith, Irish language and forms of traditional Irish music and dance provided the obvious vehicles for this Irish-Ireland movement. But, at a time when athleticism and patriotism were being linked throughout Europe and the colonies, sport was also seized upon as a means of generating a sense of Gaelic pride.

Ironically, it was the British themselves who created the precedent for linking sport with nationalism, demonstrating throughout the Empire that sport could be both a valuable stimulant to national sentiment and a useful tool for strengthening colonial domination. Wherever the Union Jack flew, the rhetoric of the public school playing field was invoked as a metaphor for British moral superiority. In Dublin too the British way of doing things was symbolised by an affinity with certain sports and games and the style in which they were played (West, 1991). It was in the face of the British attempt to commandeer the high ground of popular culture in Ireland that a counter-revolution in Gaelic sports took shape. The use of Gaelic sport as an antidote to English cultural influences was first suggested by the Young Ireland Movement. Equally concerned that sport in Ireland was becoming the prerogative of anglophiles, the I.R.B. were another political group which promoted the idea of using athletics to boost Irish nationalism. At the same time, leading figures in the Catholic Church were protesting at the popularity of pastimes which were rooted in English traditions to the detriment of Irish games. These diverse threads of resistance to the spread of English recreational habits were pulled together with the formation of the G.A.A. in 1884, which, in the words of Corry, 'was to be used in the intellectual warfare between two cultures' (Corry, 1989: 10).

The driving force behind the formation of the G.A.A. was Michael Cusack. He was a complex character who did not have a clear political manifesto. Cusack had many links with Anglo-Ireland, including participation in sports such as cricket and rugby. He firmly believed in the value of organised sports. For the most part, his idealism was in tune with the founders of the modern Olympics who believed in the importance of physical fitness, amateurism, fair play and the character-building qualities of sporting competition. However, at heart Cusack was a nationalist, having taken the Fenian Oath in 1867 and committed himself to the cause of Home Rule in 1880. He was concerned that the dominance of English sports coupled with the elitist manner in which they were played, denied access to the vast majority of native Irishmen. While Cusack's own initial objectives may have been predominantly directed towards the revitalisation of Irish sports for Irish people, the same cannot be said of several of the organisation's earliest patrons, including Archbishop Croke (in whose memory Croke Park, the national Gaelic stadium in Dublin, is named), Charles Parnell and Michael Davitt, all of whom, albeit in different ways, were active in the cause for Irish self-assertion and saw affiliation with the G.A.A. as a means of advancing that cause along with their own nationalist, political profiles. *The Irishman*, a left-wing nationalist weekly, welcomed the Association's formation and recommended that it receive the fullest support of Fenians and other separatist movements. For his part, Parnell was highly supportive of the G.A.A., believing that in the drive for major constitutional changes, a national organisation such as this could be a valuable power base. While the various parties involved in the formation of the G.A.A. disagreed about the route towards Irish independence, they were all agreed that this was a desirable goal and that the fledgling organisation would have an important role to play.

In a letter to Cusack, Land Leaguer Michael Davitt made plain his views concerning the value of promoting Gaelic games and pastimes:

Why should we not have our athletic festivals like other people? In this, as in so many matters, we ought to cut ourselves adrift from English rules and patronage and prevent the killing of those Celtic Sports which have been threatened with the same fate by the encroachment of Saxon custom as that which menaces our nationality under alien rule. (Puirseal, 1982: 45)

In a nation deeply influenced by religion, the patronage and active involvement of the Catholic Church was vital to the success of a movement which hoped to model itself on a well-established parish structure. Detailing his acceptance of Cusack's offer of patronage, Archbishop Croke spelt out, in the strongest terms, his views with regard to the purpose of the G.A.A.. Croke's ideals were striking in their combination of the distinctively English themes of rational recreation and muscular Christianity with a version of ecclesiastical, Celtic nationalism:

> Ball playing, hurling, foot-ball kicking, according to Irish rules, casting, leaping in various ways, wrestling, handy-grips, top-pegging, leap-frog, rounders, tip-in-the-hat and all such favourite exercises and amusements amongst men and boys, may now be said to be not only dead and buried but in several locations to be entirely forgotten and unknown. . . . If we continue travelling for the next score years in the same direction that we have taken for some time past, condemning the sports that were practised by our forefathers, effacing our national features, as though we were ashamed of them, and putting on, with England's stuff and broadcloths, her mashier habits and other effeminate follies as she may recommend, we had better at once and publicly abjure our nationality, clap hands for joy at the sight of the Union Jack, and place 'England's bloody red' exultantly above the green. (ibid.: 50)

The principles underlying Croke's sermonising were incorporated into the organisation's charter, which clearly endorsed the struggle for a free and united Ireland. The G.A.A.'s first charter was drawn up in an upstairs room in a hotel in Thurles, County Tipperary in 1884. It committed the organisation's members to the cause of Irish nationhood and, as the following opening extract from the modern rule book indicates, the G.A.A. continues to be committed to the same broad aims:

> The Association is a National Organisation which has as its basic aims, the strengthening of the National Identity in a 32 county Ireland through the preservation and promotion of Gaelic Games and pastimes. The Association further seeks to achieve its objectives through the active support of Irish Culture, with a constant emphasis on the importance of the preservation of the Irish language and its greater use in the life of the Nation; and in the development of a community spirit, to foster an awareness and love of the national ideals in the people of Ireland. (G.A.A., 1991)

In support of these aims, the G.A.A. included a series of regulations specifically designed to prevent the influence of foreign games and pastimes. First, there was the police rule which effectively barred the security forces from membership of the G.A.A.; second, there was the boycott rule which extended the Fenian strategy of severing economic ties with things British to the censure of sporting events organised under the auspices of English federations; finally, there was the foreign games rule

which expelled members of the G.A.A. who were discovered participating in, or indeed watching, any games which were not ethnically Irish
or which were not organised by the G.A.A.. In the early days, under
Cusack's stewardship, the Association was open to participation by
people of all religious and political persuasions, but its introduction of
these rules and its increasingly extreme nationalistic character rendered
the G.A.A. an inhospitable environment for Protestants and Unionists
(de Búrca, 1980: 27). The spirit of these regulations has been articulated
as the Ban Policy and although the three rules outlined above have been
modified or even revoked in the Irish Republic, it is within the spirit of
the Ban that the G.A.A. continues to operate, particularly north of the
border, and especially in its dealings with members of the British security
forces.

There is a mythological dimension to the G.A.A. which is rooted in
a vision of Celtic Ireland and is similar in certain respects to the *Volk-
gemeinschaft* which formed the cultural backcloth to the rise of the Third
Reich in Germany in the first quarter of the twentieth century. In this
vision, high emphasis is placed upon the purity of the Gaelic race. Gaels
are portrayed as being intellectually and physically superior to their
English counterparts, who are perceived as the product of centuries of
inter-racial mixing involving the Ancient Britons, the Romans and several
other European tribes. The racial undertones of the Gaelic movement are
well summed up in the *Gaelic Annual* of 1907–1908, which declared:

> The Irish Celt is distinguished among the races for height and strength, manly
> vigour and womanly grace; despite wars and domestic disabilities, the stamina
> of the race has survived in almost pristine perfection. The ideal Gael is a
> matchless athlete, sober, pure in mind, speech and deed, self-possessed, self-
> reliant, self-respecting, loving his religion and his country with a deep and
> restless love, earnest in thought and effective in action. (Corry, 1989: 87)

In many ways this type of racist rhetoric was a reaction against the
xenophobia of Victorian England which had singled out the Irish for
derision and which, in satirical magazines such as *Punch*, caricatured the
Irish as being physically and mentally inferior to those of Anglo Saxon
stock. For the land of saints and scholars this was too much to bear and
the wholesale revival of Gaelic cultural traditions, including sports, was
an attempt to create a more positive image which, regardless of stereotypes accepted elsewhere, would enhance self-esteem in the Irish
themselves.

Despite the blatant anti-Englishness which fuelled the emergence of the
G.A.A., a characteristically British approach to sports was used by the
organisation's founder members to breathe life into otherwise dormant
traditional Gaelic pastimes. Indeed, despite the ethnocentric ambitions of

Cusack and Croke and the republican politics of the I.R.B., no sporting development at this stage could avoid the influence of English organisational practices. As Mandle suggests, 'however much the Association might seek to distance itself from Anglicisation it could not escape the contemporary impact of the revolution in games-playing and games-organisation that has proved to be one of Victorian England's most enduring legacies' (Mandle, 1987: 14).

In this regard the birth of the G.A.A. and the codification of Gaelic sports which followed can be regarded both as a nationalist reaction against English influence and as a product of the athletic revolution which had been pioneered by the British. Thus, the ethos of the organisation hinges upon two conflicting ideologies. At the overtly political level the G.A.A. is essentially Irish and nationalist, whereas at the purely sporting level there are obvious parallels with the British emphasis on the moral, physical and character-building qualities of organised sport as well as a strict adherence to the principles of amateurism. Nevertheless, as Mandle observes, 'the fact remains that this organisation, created to oppose all that Britain stood for could not avoid the consequences of its particular location in time and space' (ibid.: 15).

Thus, of Ireland's many and varied sporting organisations, the G.A.A. has the most obvious political pedigree. During its first decade, to use Cusack's own words, 'the Association spread through the country like a prairie fire', but not necessarily for the largely sporting reasons which he had originally envisaged. Commenting on this, John Bowman in *The Sunday Times* (23 April 1989) is correct when he states that 'it [the G.A.A.] is one of the few examples of success of the Irish-Ireland movement whose aim at the turn of the century was nothing less than to undo the anglicisation of Ireland in language, culture and politics'. However, the political dimension which runs through the G.A.A. is both subtle and complex, reflecting the nuances of Irish politics in general, both in terms of relationships with Britain and in terms of manifest divisions within the nationalist community itself. At the time of the Association's inception, while there was a groundswell of opinion in favour of Home Rule, the route to that objective was controversial, with nationalist politics broadly divided into two recognisable camps, both present within the ranks of the G.A.A..

On one side, with Parnell as a figure-head, there were those who favoured more or less peaceful, constitutional methods to bring about independence. On the other, were those who rallied to the call of the I.R.B. and who advocated the use of physical force alongside political agitation as the more direct means to secure a free Irish Republic. Parnell's supporters were in the majority within the G.A.A. during its formative years, and as a consequence, the organisation suffered almost terminally in the wake of the O'Shea scandal, an affair of the heart

which cost Parnell his political career and seriously damaged the constitu-
tionalists' platform. The degree of affection for Parnell within the G.A.A.
was amply demonstrated at his funeral in 1891 when six members carried
his coffin and thousands of others, brandishing black draped hurley
sticks, marched with the cortege in one of the largest political gatherings
ever witnessed in Dublin. Not long afterwards, there was an equal display
of political and athletic unity when the G.A.A. and the I.R.B. jointly
organised the funeral of Pat McNally, a G.A.A. member who had died
in prison after being sentenced for treason because of his political
activities. Once more, thousands of G.A.A. members lined the streets of
Dublin as McNally's coffin passed by, followed by a march past of the
entire membership council of the G.A.A.. In the light of such demonstrations, it is not surprising that the British authorities in Dublin Castle began
to associate the Gaelic movement with Irish Republicanism.

Despite such public displays of unity, political in-fighting between
these two factions and the added interference of the Catholic Church
threatened the survival of the Association during its formative years.
Because of the potential of the G.A.A. to mobilise mass support, from
its very inception the control of the Association became a prominent
feature of the factional struggle between the various elements of Irish
nationalism. Indeed, in the last decades of the nineteenth century the
fledgling movement was almost ripped apart through internecine conflict
between the I.R.B., constitutional nationalists and the Catholic Church.
By 1888, the latter was actively campaigning against the G.A.A.
throughout Ireland because of the I.R.B.'s leading role in the Association. Nevertheless, some leading churchmen, such as Croke, continued to
believe that the G.A.A. was worth fighting for (Mandle, 1987: 63).
Largely due to the influence of the Catholic Church, however, the
G.A.A.'s close association with Parnell cost the organisation dearly after
his fall and the number of affiliated clubs dropped from 1,000 in 1888
to 220 in 1892 (Corry, 1989: 37). All of this political squabbling deflected
the central council's attention away from the administration of the
Association, which became a shambles and undermined the popular
appeal of Gaelic sports. This taught a lesson to a minority of 'the more
far-sighted of the men who were trying to keep the association alive'
(Puirseal, 1982: 103), a lesson which has served them and their successors
well – namely, to be committed to nationalist goals in the broadest sense,
but not to affiliate the G.A.A. to any single political party or overtly
political expedient.

Without such a guiding maxim having being established, the G.A.A.
survived the cataclysmic events of the first quarter of the twentieth
century only with great difficulty. The organisation's move towards a
non-party political platform was by no means smooth. By 1914, many of
the younger members of the G.A.A. had joined Sinn Fein and the Irish

Volunteer Movement, turning their backs on the constitutionalist politics of the National Party. In January of that year, the Association's President, James Nowlan, came out in their support, calling upon members to 'join the Volunteers and learn to shoot straight' (Corry, 1989: 96). However, in keeping with the G.A.A.'s desire to distance itself from formal political involvement, Croke Park was refused to the Volunteers for drilling purposes in the same month. Nevertheless, collectively and individually, certain Gaelic sportsmen were prominent in the events leading up to and surrounding the Republican rising of Easter 1916. Several Easter insurrectionists who were prominent members of the G.A.A. were arrested and executed, including Padraig Pearse, Sean McDermott, Con Colbert, Michael O'Hanrahan and Eamonn Ceannt. The British clearly believed that the G.A.A., as one of the most prominent nationalist bodies in the country, was guilty of complicity in the rebellion. Throughout Ireland thousands of Gaels were arrested and interned by the British, including Nowlan himself (Puirseal, 1982: 168–9). Indeed, so many prominent Gaelic players were interned that the 1916 final of the Wolfe Tone Tournament between Kerry and Louth was played in Frongoch Prison Camp in Wales (Corry, 1989: 102–3).

Generally, while the Easter rising came as a shock to the Irish people, it failed as an immediate spark to revolution. It was the ruthless manner in which the British put down the rebellion, dealt with its perpetrators and continued to repress the people which gradually turned the minority struggle for independence into a popular cause. The G.A.A. had been implicated in the events of 1916, after which it became the object of intensive surveillance and harassment at the hands of the police and military. The British mistrust and dislike for the G.A.A. was made brutally manifest on 'Bloody Sunday', 20 November 1920.

During 1920, the sporting activities of the Association had all but been suspended while a bitter and bloody guerrilla war ensued between forces of the crown and a coalition of Irish Republicans. However, late in the autumn, the Tipperary board issued a challenge to Dublin and a crowd in excess of 10,000 turned out to watch the resulting match at Croke Park on 20 November. As the match got underway, a large force of British Army auxiliaries, known as the Black and Tans, scaled the walls of the ground and began shooting into the crowd causing them to stampede for cover. In the ensuing mêlée, 13 people were killed, including the captain of the Tipperary side, Michael Hogan, and three children. It soon became obvious that the Croke Park incident was in response to events which had occurred earlier that day, when Republicans had assassinated 14 British secret service agents and two members of the Royal Irish Constabulary at various locations in Dublin. Officially explained as a routine security operation that went wrong, the Croke Park massacre was interpreted by the majority of people as a wilful act of punishment and revenge. This incident is etched in the consciousness of Gaels and was commemorated by the naming of one of Croke Park's stands after the dead Tipperary captain. 'Bloody Sunday' and operations like it rapidly accelerated the alienation felt between the authorities and the Irish people, seriously undermining the basis for continued British rule over Ireland. It was only two years after 'Bloody Sunday' that pressure from home and abroad persuaded the British Parliament to grant a degree of independence to Ireland in 1921.

The main qualification to the 1921 Act of Parliament, which granted Irish independence and established the Irish Free State, was an arrangement through which the six counties in the north east of the country remained under British rule. From the perspective of the politics of the G.A.A. the partition of Ireland had three outcomes.

First, there was the civil war which briefly, but violently, divided the Free State between those who accepted the Treaty and advocated political initiatives to bring about reunification, and those who rejected the Treaty and supported the continuation of the armed struggle until the whole of the island was free. As an organisation which had been a symbol for the struggle for independence, the G.A.A. found itself caught up in the civil conflict. As an official body it carefully avoided affiliation to either camp, but the Association's membership was riven by pro-Treaty and anti-Treaty factions, and throughout 1922 and 1923 sporting competitions were largely suspended as sporting interests were subsumed by the civil war.

Second, towards the end of the conflict, the G.A.A. was called upon to play a mediating role. While this initiative was not in itself particularly successful, it anticipated the important integrative function which the Association assumed once hostilities ceased. The civil war ended formally in 1923, but deep resentments remained throughout the 26 counties. Operating in hundreds of parishes throughout the country, the G.A.A. served as neutral territory within which a common sense of national identity could be rebuilt. In this regard, the organisation in the south found its pre-political function more or less inverted from a traditional position of antagonism towards the state to that of cultural and ideological supporter. Whereas the G.A.A. had been formed in the 1880s as part of a campaign of resistance against English hegemony, by the late 1920s it had become a vital part of the institutional infrastructure of the fledgling Irish Free State. To this end, in its more recent history, the movement has been eagerly embraced by leading constitutional politicians intent on securing stability within the new regime. The annual all-Ireland hurling and football finals held at Croke Park are both sporting competitions and festivals of national self-determination. As such, while attendance at national soccer and rugby matches may be optional, the presence of senior politicians at G.A.A. finals is virtually mandatory.

Thirdly, however, as the oppositional political dimension of the G.A.A. in the Republic disappeared, north of the border its controversial political profile has remained high. At no time has Northern Ireland, as a political entity, achieved total acceptance from the minority Irish Catholic population and, in continued support for the cause of Irish unity, the G.A.A. has gone on playing a political role.

In 1969, in the face of the intransigence of the Ulster Unionist Party, the constitutional political expression of loyalist Protestantism, and as a result of the denial of civil rights to Catholics, general dissent and sporadic violence began to give way to a more concerted campaign of Republican opposition. The resultant Troubles have established a pattern of political life against which all aspects of Northern Irish society, including sports, must be viewed. While the formal political and military circumstances of the Troubles capture the headlines, the battle for cultural supremacy has been no less fierce. In this contest the G.A.A. plays its traditional role, asserting Irish national distinctiveness and espousing the cause of Irish freedom from a society run by the British and their Ulster Protestant agents.

In this regard, the general situation of the G.A.A. in Northern Ireland, particularly since the Troubles, closely resembles that of the organisation shortly after it was established more than a hundred years ago. As we have seen, however, around the turn of the century the G.A.A. learned that while it was important to have a rhetorical commitment to Irish nationalism, to adopt one political strategy in favour of another could have proved fatal to the Association. Thus, in the North, while individual members may actively support a variety of violent and non-violent political organisations, as a body the G.A.A. remains officially neutral. This was the case in 1981 during the Republican prisoners' hunger strikes. The intensity of support for the prisoners was clearly expressed by individual Gaelic clubs for example, and in advertisements taken out in local newspapers, without the organisation as a whole being implicated in political activism.

Peter Quinn, who was appointed to the Presidency of the G.A.A. in 1991, has vigorously denied that his organisation promotes political division in Northern Ireland. A year before his election as President, speaking in his capacity of Chairman of the Ulster Board at a conference on sport and community relations, he suggested that the G.A.A. merely reflected existing divisions, the responsibilities for which lay outside the boundaries of sport:

> We cannot be held accountable for the fragmentation of society in this part of our island. To attempt to make sport, especially Gaelic sport, the scapegoat for the failures of politicians and for those paid to manage society and the economy is dangerous, if not hypocritical. (*Belfast Telegraph*, 30 June 1989)

However, behind such statements it is clear that the G.A.A. is operating with a very narrow definition of politics. The fact that the G.A.A. eschews formal links with political organisations does not mean that it is apolitical. It is significant that while the practice of conducting the formal aspects of provincial council meetings in the Irish language has been discontinued in Leinster, Munster and Connaught, it persists in Ulster (Corry, 1989: 89). Before formal political positions can be articulated by both constitutional and non-constitutional means, individuals and groups must develop political identities through a variety of social and cultural associations. The range of nationalist political outlets in Northern Ireland, from the Social and Democratic Labour Party (S.D.L.P.) through to the Provisional I.R.A., is grounded in an affiliation to a heritage which is clearly Irish rather than British. The G.A.A. is unabashed in its desire to promote Irish nationalism and it is in this regard that it must be seen as a powerful player in the politics of Northern Ireland.

Indeed, the nationalism symbolised by the Association presents a dilemma to the British Government and its representatives in the Province. Following a liberal-democratic tradition which values rational recreation, and informed by general theories about the positive role sport can play in defusing community tension and social conflict, Westminster politicians have been willing to recognise the G.A.A.'s value as a stabilising force in the nationalist community and are persuaded to treat it like any other popular sport in the United Kingdom. At the very least, Gaelic games provide a vehicle through which young Catholics can expend energies which otherwise might be harnessed to more overtly political ends. Young men in particular are believed to be especially vulnerable to the temptation of the excitement and status perceived to be offered by the paramilitaries in Northern Ireland. Because of the nationalist orientation of the Association, participation in the G.A.A. can provide young men with relatively safe opportunities to display their nationalist credentials in ways which do not directly threaten their own well-being or that of the state. As such, Gaelic sport can be tolerated as a safety mechanism.

Secondly, in the light of initiatives such as the Anglo-Irish Agreement, a treaty which purports to foster better cross-border relationships, there is a certain logic to the British Government's support for the north-south affiliations promoted by the G.A.A.. Unfair treatment of this organisation, on the other hand, would be seen as indicative of a deep-seated unwillingness by the British to sanction an Irish dimension in Ulster, even at the level of popular culture. For these reasons, the activities of the G.A.A. are supported by one branch of the British state and are funded through the Department of Education and the Sports Council. As Knox (1989: 149) points out, between 1962 and 1982, much to the annoyance of Unionist politicians, the G.A.A. in Northern Ireland received £819,000 in grant aid from these sources. Paradoxically, however, the amount of funding they receive is restricted owing to the fact that membership of the G.A.A. is not open to members of the police or the security forces in Northern Ireland (rule 15), a fact commented on by East Belfast's Democratic Unionist M.P., Peter Robinson:

> It is intolerable that the government, accepting the G.A.A. does discriminate and arguing that such action is repugnant, should aid, induce and incite this association to further discrimination. An immediate reversal of this policy is demanded. (ibid.: 149)

The exclusion clause is interpreted by loyalists as evidence that the G.A.A. continues to be committed to the struggle for full national independence. This interpretation tends to be shared by the targets of rule 15, the security forces themselves. Thus, while one part of the British state sponsors this organisation, in other areas of government the G.A.A. is viewed with considerable suspicion and its activities are monitored accordingly.

In a context bordering on civil war, where cultural preferences are reasonable indicators of political leanings, it is not surprising that the G.A.A. attracts the attention of the British Army, which operates in Northern Ireland with a mandate to detect and neutralise, as far as possible, the enemy within. Surveillance of individual G.A.A. members, along with their clubs, is based on the premise that although they may be meeting for the purposes of sport, by their membership of the G.A.A. they have proclaimed a nationalist political preference. In this way their sporting involvement is viewed as a political statement. Thus, while sports such as hockey, rugby and soccer are largely ignored by soldiers, the G.A.A. constantly finds its activities disrupted by them. Disruption includes stopping and searching G.A.A. members travelling to and from games and meetings, raiding games in progress and the establishment of more permanent structures of vigilance, often involving the construction of army and police barracks on or adjacent to Gaelic pitches. The best known examples of the latter have been the temporary occupation of Casement Park, the Provincial G.A.A. headquarters in west Belfast, and the permanent security forces' installation built on playing fields belonging to the G.A.A. in Crossmaglen, South Armagh. The official explanation in cases such as these is that the land and the sites are the most appropriate vantage points for military installations. Nevertheless, there is a strong feeling in nationalist circles that the main reason behind such incursions is a policy directed towards undermining the morale of the local population by violating their national games. Thus, what is viewed as necessary policing by the security forces in Northern Ireland, is seen as provocative sectarian harassment by the G.A.A..

Certainly, Gaelic sport in Northern Ireland is more than a game and has come to be recognised by both sides as a reservoir of Irish identity. In keeping with a siege mentality established many centuries ago, Protestants in Northern Ireland come to regard individual members of the G.A.A. not merely as potential trouble-makers, but as representatives of an alien tradition which threatens the Protestant and Unionist way of life. The constitutional position of the G.A.A., concerning the unification of Ireland and the exclusion of the security forces, does nothing to alleviate such suspicions. Neither does the naming of the Provincial stadium after the Republican hero and British traitor, Sir Roger Casement or the continued practice of using hurley sticks to symbolise Irish nationalism, together with their use as weapons by paramilitary punishment squads. (The latter is a practice which has been discontinued by the I.R.A. after complaints by nationalists inside and outside the G.A.A. that the organisation's image was being tarnished. The fact that punishment squads have taken to using baseball bats to carry out their work is an ironic response to the sensitivities of the Irish sporting purists.) In addition, many games are played under the flag of the Irish Republic, preceded by the Irish national anthem, which confirms for Ulster Protestants that the activities of the G.A.A. are no less than the thin end of the wedge of a campaign to bring about the unification of Ireland under Dublin rule.

Local members of the predominantly Protestant security forces, brought up in the shadow of such traditions, are bound to be negatively influenced in their routine dealings with those who bear affiliation to the G.A.A.. In turn, this must effect the attitude of visiting troops. British soldiers may not themselves be inherently hostile to what is for them just another sport. However, the collaboration of troops from Glasgow, Liverpool, Birmingham and London, and locally recruited members of the security forces, notably in the Ulster Defence Regiment (U.D.R.) and the Royal Ulster Constabulary (R.U.C.), means that the inherent, but objective, suspicion of the military can easily fall prey to the powerful and indigenous sectarian currents which view the G.A.A. and Republicanism as one and the same thing. This certainly did not go unnoticed in nationalist circles when in 1988 Aiden McAnespie was shot dead by a British soldier while crossing the border on the way to play Gaelic football. This was interpreted by nationalists in the same way as the Croke Park massacre in 1920. Neither did it escape the attention of loyalists that at McAnespie's funeral the drape for his coffin was a Gaelic football jersey. The latter was viewed by many loyalists as a barely disguised expression of Irish nationalism, even if family and friends sought only to testify to the dead man's sporting enthusiasm.

It is not only the security forces who mistrust the G.A.A. and link them with Republicanism. Loyalist politicians on occasions have sought to use their authority to obstruct the development of the Association and its activities in the Province. Annoyed by the financial support which the G.A.A. gets from the British Government, certain Unionist councils have adopted other tactics to disrupt Gaelic sport. For example, for many years the Craigavon Borough Council refused to grant St Peter's Club a lease for land upon which to develop a complex for Gaelic sports and pastimes. The land in question was next to Brownlow House, the head-quarters of the Royal Black Preceptory, one of the more significant institutions of Protestantism in Northern Ireland. The councillors claimed that to permit games to be played on Sunday, in the shadow of this establishment, would be particularly offensive to local Protestants and refused development permission. Not satisfied with this ruling, the Club took the Council to the High Court and won its case. The Council was obliged to pay legal costs which amounted to a sum in excess of £100,000. In summing up, Lord Chief Justice Lowry indicated that the heavy financial penalty had been imposed because the council members who had prevented the development of St Peter's had been motivated by sectarian bitterness (Knox, 1989).

Likewise, in 1980 there was uproar in Londonderry after the City Council had granted planning permission for two Gaelic football pitches in the Protestant area of the Waterside. In a display of unity, the Official Unionist Party (O.U.P.) and the Democratic Unionist Party (D.U.P.) were joined by loyalist paramilitary groups and leading Protestant Church figures in condemning the Council's decision. The issue of the Gaelic pitches on the Waterside was deliberately used by a Protestant coalition to jeopardise the power-sharing arrangements which had been worked out between certain unionist and nationalist members of the City Council. After considerable disruption of Council business a second site for the pitches was chosen, but because this was still in the Waterside, local loyalist groups pressed ahead with their protests. As Knox (1989: 152) comments:

> The first match kicked off in March 1981 and a local D.U.P. Councillor who grabbed the ball in protest received a black-eye; violence ensued. D.U.P. supporters broke bottles on the pitch in an attempt to prevent Gaelic football being played and council staff refused to carry out maintenance work following threats from the Ulster Defence Association (U.D.A.).

Shortly after this incident the City Council banned all games on the site for 12 months, blaming a lack of maintenance. Since then nothing but soccer has been played there, which, for reasons which will be made clear later, is doubly infuriating for the G.A.A.. Similar incidents have been recorded throughout the Province. In Cookstown, during a debate over the provision of Gaelic football posts for council-owned playing fields, a D.U.P. councillor openly accused the G.A.A. of being a front for the Provisional I.R.A.. But it was the Rev. Ian Paisley, D.U.P. M.P. for North Antrim, who, in a dispute over the provision of Gaelic facilities in his constituency, captured popular loyalist sentiment when he stated:

> The G.A.A. hadn't a leg to stand on. Their proposal to build a Gaelic pitch in a loyalist area would be similar to me building a Free Presbyterian Church in Andersonstown (*Catholic West Belfast*) and flying the Union Jack on top of it. (Knox, 1989: 157)

In 1989 uproar was caused within Belfast City Council when the U.U.P. Lord Mayor, Reg Empey, invited the Antrim hurling team to visit the City Hall in recognition of their unprecedented success in reaching the all-Ireland hurling finals. Former Lord Mayor, D.U.P. Alderman Sammy Wilson claimed that the G.A.A. was a sectarian organisation which brought politics into sport through its refusal to accept R.U.C. men and soldiers as members. Thus, he went on to say, 'regardless of the achievements of the Antrim team, they should not be welcomed into the City Hall. All right thinking Protestants will be appalled by this invitation' (*Belfast Telegraph*, 5 September 1989). While this contrasts vividly with the cross-party support for civic receptions for County Down Gaelic footballers in the 1960s, before the start of the Troubles, it was echoed in 1991 when the same County won the all-Ireland football final in Dublin. While this was the cause of much rejoicing among Northern Ireland's Catholics, the response from many loyalists, who view with great trepidation anything described as all-Irish, was generally muted. Once more, Belfast City Council voted against hosting a civic reception for the team.

The action of Belfast's Unionist-dominated Council captured the mood of many Ulster Protestants, a minority of whom actively sought to disrupt the celebrations which took place when the coveted Sam Maguire trophy was paraded north of the border. Several trains carrying returning Down fans from Dublin to towns in Northern Ireland were stoned as they passed through loyalist neighbourhoods. Not long afterwards the clubhouse of a Gaelic club in County Down was badly damaged by an arson attack. The most extreme position was taken by the Ulster Freedom Fighters (U.F.F.), a loyalist paramilitary organisation, who issued death threats to all active G.A.A. members. In an attempt to explain their position, the U.F.F. accused the G.A.A. of acting as a front for the Provisional I.R.A.. The situation became so tense that in 1992 leading officials from the G.A.A. met with selected loyalists at a venue in the Irish Republic in an effort to persuade them that their organisation was purely a sporting body and that as such their activities, on and off the field, posed no threat to the Union. Not only Unionists, however, have expressed concern at the current image of the G.A.A.. This was encapsulated in the reaction to an episode involving the G.A.A. at the end of 1991.

On 23 October 1991, invitations were issued to the Dublin and Down County Boards to celebrate the centenary of the Clanna Gael-Fontenoys club in Dublin by playing a Gaelic football match at the Royal Dublin Showgrounds (R.D.S.), to be preceded by a League of Ireland soccer fixture involving Shamrock Rovers and Shelbourne. Both Boards initially accepted the invitation. However, the G.A.A.'s Games Committee decided on 13 November that the games should not go ahead as the venue was not a ground vested in the Association. Further discussions took place in an effort to allow the game to proceed. The Down Board, however, became unhappy that the G.A.A.'s Central Council could not give an assurance that playing at the R.D.S. on the same bill as association football would not be in conflict with the Association's rules. Peter Quinn, the Association's President, is reported to have been furious when he first heard of the proposal and was unwilling to accept the conditions which had been framed in order to permit the involvement of Gaelic sides. On 7 December the Central Council accepted that the match should be cancelled.

Numerous prominent citizens of the Irish Republic voiced their disapproval at the G.A.A.'s decision. These included the former Taoiseach, Jack Lynch, himself a legendary figure in the history of Gaelic sport. Dublin newspapers went as far as to suggest a link between the G.A.A.'s decision and the continuation of violence in Northern Ireland. Unionists, it was argued, had been given a clear message that the G.A.A. is an intransigent, sectarian body which they were right to view with suspicion. While this would not be an accurate picture of the Association as a whole, some officials involved in making the decision about the proposed R.D.S. fixture, including Mr Quinn from Northern Ireland, made it appear so:

> It seems clear that the objection to the proposed venture was a deep-seated prejudice by some senior people in the G.A.A., many of them from Northern Ireland, against what they continue to regard as a 'foreign game'. Situated in the context of Northern Ireland, this view has a particularly forceful resonance. (*Sunday Tribune*, 15 December 1991)

Although the attitudes of Northern G.A.A. officials are understandably different from those of their Southern counterparts since they are obliged to operate in a different political context, it was felt to be 'a pity that such sectariansim should be largely imposed on the G.A.A. in the south by a hard-line element, infused with the dangerous passions of the north' (ibid.). Among county secretaries canvassed for their views on the R.D.S. game, two of the three who took a hard-line attitude were from the North – Padraig Donnelly from Quinn's own county Fermanagh and Gerard Fagan of Armagh. (The other secretary opposed to the fixture was Liam Creaven of Meath (ibid.).) Indeed, the hard-line stance of the northerners was reinforced at the G.A.A.'s annual congress in April 1992 when a motion proposed by the Sligo Board advocating multiple use of G.A.A. grounds and allowing for sharing arrangements with rugby and soccer, was heavily defeated.

Overall, the whole incident and the responses to it would support our argument that of necessity the G.A.A. now plays two radically different roles in Irish cultural and political life. In the Irish Republic its role is complicated by the fact that it must now compete with other sports, notably soccer, for the right to be regarded as the 'national' game, whereas for northern Gaels the only truly 'nationalist' sports remain those peculiar to Ireland. In this respect there was one other no less important factor in the R.D.S. controversy. One of the main aims of the whole enterprise was to enhance the profile of Gaelic games in south Dublin where the Fontenoys club is based. Gaelic clubs have problems throughout the capital city and this is particularly true on the southside where both rugby and soccer are popular. By adopting a purist position, therefore, and preventing this joint fixture, Gaelic officials lost an opportunity to promote their sport. Indeed, their attitudes may have simply endorsed existing feelings that the G.A.A. is an anachronistic and introspective sporting body and that more global sports such as rugby and soccer have considerably more appeal in modern Ireland.

Thus, the truth of the matter may be that the main problem currently facing the G.A.A. is neither the intransigence of Unionist politicians in Northern Ireland, nor entanglement within the formal politics of division in general. Rather, it is the growing threat posed on both sides of the border by the popularity of the other codes of football, particularly soccer. The success of the Irish national soccer team under the management of Jack Charlton in the 1988 European Championships and the 1990 World Cup has given a massive boost to the profile of a sport which was already on an upward curve. While the claims made by the founder members of the G.A.A. at the turn of the last century, that association football was essentially an English game, had a degree of plausibility, as we approach the turn of the next, soccer is beyond question a universal game with global popular appeal. Despite concerted advertising campaigns on television and in the newspapers, when senior politicians openly rejoice at the nation's success in soccer, it is difficult for the G.A.A. to convince today's generation of Irish games players that choosing association football over Gaelic games is a betrayal of their national heritage. As Bowman remarks:

In the middle term they [the G.A.A.] must be concerned at the appeal of televised world-class soccer. Ireland is one of the few countries where three codes of football prosper. But it would be naive to presume that all three can prosper indefinitely. Many astute observers reckon that the threat must be to Gaelic football. (*The Sunday Times*, 23 April 1989)

This view is supported by *The Irish Times* columnist, Michael Finlan, who recognises the growing cultural power of soccer throughout Ireland, believing that it is well on the way to usurping the authority of the G.A.A. and becoming the national sport:

We do seem to have reached the stage where soccer, a once-reviled symbol of foreign yokes and repression, is threatening to become *the* national game of Ireland. And – oh the shame of it! – it's all largely the work of an Englishman who has cast a wonder-working spell on an Irish team which has some members who'd have trouble identifying a shamrock and might punch you out for using swear words if you tried the *cupla focail* [native language] on them. (*The Irish Times*, 8 June 1990)

As Finlan suggests, it must be particularly worrying for the G.A.A. that this is happening at a time when, with an English management team and a large proportion of current international players having been born in Britain, the influence of the British on the development of the game in Ireland is stronger now than at any time since the last century. Undoubtedly, the main reasons why many gifted young Irish sportsmen such as Niall Quinn, Kevin Moran and Frank Stapleton opted to play soccer instead of Gaelic is that soccer afforded them the opportunity to display and test their abilities in an international arena and earn a good living. Furthermore, the country's participation in international soccer tournaments provides the whole nation with an opportunity to join in the promotion of Ireland on the world stage. While an all-Ireland Gaelic final at Croke Park may have the status of a national institution, it cannot rival an appearance by the Republic of Ireland in the quarter-finals of the soccer World Cup as an occasion for mass celebration. In addition, and despite the political considerations to be discussed in the next chapter, the G.A.A. has lost some of its best players to rugby union. Notable Irish rugby internationals, such as Moss Keane, have represented their counties at Gaelic football. In nationalist circles, the switch from Gaelic to such a characteristically English game is tanta-mount to treason, but it should be remembered that the Republic's first and longest serving President, Eamon de Valera, was a passionate follower of rugby union.

In recent years the insularity of the G.A.A. has been further threatened by the emergence of the game of 'compromise rules' football. This, as the name suggests, involves the bringing together of two different codes of football: Gaelic and Australian Rules. The rationale behind this development is directed towards the facilitation of international competition between Ireland and Australia. Many within the ranks of the organisation object to this development for practical reasons, arguing that despite superficial similarities, in terms of strategies, techniques and overall structure, the two games are in fact quite different. It is argued that by encouraging its better players to play both Gaelic and 'compromise rules', the G.A.A. is unintentionally lowering the overall standards of the native game. Others argue that this lowering of standards is accelerated through the recruitment into the professional Australian Football League of those Gaelic players who are successful in compromise rules test matches between the two countries. However, the staunchest resistance to compromise rules comes from traditionalists within the G.A.A. who argue that the whole concept of the internationalisation of Gaelic games is anathema to the organisation's reason for being: the promotion of a distinctively Irish physical culture. 'Compromise rules' football is viewed as a dilution of the ethnic pedigree of Gaelic games and as such a threat to the cause of Irish nationalism.

Another objection to 'compromise rules' is that, given the highly developed spirit of commercial enterprise which surrounds the Australian game, elements of professionalism will contaminate the amateur ethos which has been one of the G.A.A.'s most important guiding principles for more than a hundred years. The strict amateurism of the G.A.A. has also been threatened by the establishment of Gaelic sports clubs in the United States. These clubs, which are less concerned about amateurism than their Irish conterparts, eagerly recruit players from Ireland and pay them generously for their services. This is in keeping with a universal trend away from strict adherence to amateurism across a wide range of sports, most notably within Olympic circles. At the higher levels of participation, association football has been openly professional for many years, as has cricket. In 1990 a former citadel of amateurism, the English Rugby Football Union, initiated a process which allows leading rugby players to receive financial benefits from their involvement in the sport, and many believe this to be the beginning of the end of amateur rugby union in the British Isles. In this regard, the G.A.A. is looking increasingly isolated in its stand against professionalism. It is ironic that as we approach the turn of the twentieth century, an organisation which was established to resist the domination of English sporting ideology has become one of the last defenders of those Corinthian principles which are so bound up with the English public school tradition.

That the G.A.A. has a political dimension is undeniable. However, as we have argued, the nature of its politicisation is complex, the understanding of which requires an insight into the relationship between

culture and politics. In its most visible guise, politics is no more than the
formal expression of social interests in a context of intergroup conflict.
Social interests, such as class consciousness, feminism or nationalism,
have to be nurtured through collective association and shared sentiment
before they can be mobilised in the formal political arena. The mobilisation and strengthening of nationalism in a 32-county Ireland continues to
be one of the most important objectives of the Association, bringing it
into clear conflict with the aims and aspirations of the loyalist population
and their defenders in the North. In this regard, while we may accept
that as a body the G.A.A. is not directly involved with any particular
strand of Irish Republicanism, the often-voiced claim of its officials, that
the Association is apolitical, seems highly spurious.

The G.A.A. was formed at a time when Irish national assertion was
growing along a broad front involving both political and cultural formations. At its inception the Association was imbued with a dual purpose:
to promote specifically Irish sports and pastimes; and to mobilise the
mass of the population in the cause of a united and independent Ireland.
The strength of the G.A.A. has been that working towards the former
inevitably has furthered the aims of the latter. In developing an all-
Ireland network of Gaelic sports clubs and sponsoring a series of leagues
and competitions, in its time, the G.A.A. has considerably advanced the
separate identity of the Irish people. Reviewing the Association's history
up to 1924, Mandle leaves us in no doubt as to its importance in this
respect:

> It is arguable that no organisation had done more for Irish nationalism than
> the GAA – not the IRB, so influential in its founding but now dissolved, not
> the Gaelic League, its linguistic counterpart which had failed in its mission to
> restore the national language, not the Irish Parliamentary Party, which had
> been unable to adjust to the nationalist revival, not even Sinn Fein, which had
> broken apart under the impact of the treaty. (Mandle, 1987: 221)

Before independence and partition in 1921, the G.A.A. was one of the
sturdiest cultural foundations upon which more formalised strategies of
political opposition to British rule were constructed. While individual
members had serious differences in terms of which strategies were most
appropriate, the G.A.A., as an organisation, while being avowedly
nationalist, adopted a neutral political profile. This enabled it to act as
a valuable structure for mediation and national integration once
independence was secured and the border issue had subsided. As such,
in the 26 counties of the Republic, since its establishment, the G.A.A.
has moved from being a focus of opposition to the British State in
Ireland to being one of the most important structures of institutional
support for the Irish Free State, and later the Irish Republic, outside of
the Catholic Church.

At present, however, the pre-1921 function of the G.A.A. remains largely the same in Northern Ireland, where it serves as a reservoir for Irish identity in a complex contest for hegemony involving the multiple institutions of the British state, various groupings of loyalists and a range of nationalist political and cultural organisations. The political presence of the G.A.A. in the Province is reinforced by regular interference into its affairs by the security forces and Unionist politicians. Under such circumstances, and true to its charter, it is unlikely that the G.A.A. will soften its line on nationalism in the North until some far-reaching political solution for the Troubles has been achieved. Undoubtedly, to interest the G.A.A., such a solution would have to revisit the vexed issue of partition and, as Peter Lennon of the *Guardian* (7 September 1989) remarks, 'the day an RUC man turns up at a local GAA club, no doubt sporting an orange sash with union jack patterned shorts and socks, will no doubt be the day that heralds the unification of Ireland'. At the time of writing, the prospect of the security forces being welcomed by the G.A.A. and the vision of a united Ireland appear equally far-fetched.

3

BRITISH SPORTS AND IRISH IDENTITY

It is undeniable that Ireland had its own sporting tradition which pre-dated the plantation and the introduction of British colonial rule. Never-theless, as we have seen, the massive revival in Gaelic games was spearheaded by the G.A.A. as a direct response to the successful introduction of British sports and pastimes. Cricket, rugby union and, to a lesser extent, field hockey are thriving reminders of the international influence exerted by Britain during the age of empire. Although rugby is now played in every continent, the countries in which it is played by most people and at the highest level are, with the exception of France, those which formed parts of the Empire. Cricket has been even less successful than rugby in broadening its appeal beyond the boundaries of former British influence. Although hockey has become established as a mainstream sport in countries like Germany and Holland, it remains a major sport throughout the British Commonwealth. The willingness of people to carry on with these British games, even after political independence, might be taken to indicate a vestigial reverence for the institutions and traditions of the mother country. To a certain extent this is true, but it is also the case that former colonies regard a sporting contest with Britain/England as a symbolic opportunity to emphasise that independence by showing through victory that they are more learned than the teacher. It appears to have been accepted that the best way to achieve this is to compete at those sports which most epitomise Englishness – hence, the passion in the West Indies or the Indian sub-continent for cricket or the enthusiasm for cricket and rugby in Australia and New Zealand. What is striking is the fact that, in contrast to Ireland, none of these former colonies decided to institutionalise their national independence by rejecting these 'British' sports and pursuing indigenous pastimes instead.

Through the re-establishment of Gaelic games, the Irish pursued a policy of sporting national self-determination which is rare. The only worthwhile comparisons are to be made with Australian Rules Football (which still has to compete at home with 'British' sports to be regarded as a major vehicle for the expression of Australian sporting defiance) and, more pertinently, baseball and American football in the United States and ice hockey in Canada, which are national games with only indirect links to, essentially, British pastimes. Unlike the situation in Canada or the United States, however, British games, like cricket, rugby and hockey, have continued to flourish alongside native sport in Ireland. This chapter examines the role of these games in Ireland and asks whether they have succeeded in maintaining an apolitical profile or if, like Gaelic sport, they are not only influenced by political divisions in Ireland but have themselves helped to foster these divisions.

CRICKET

In spite of its quintessential Englishness, cricket continues to be played in both parts of Ireland and not merely in that part which remains within the United Kingdom. Indeed, the existence of the border has made no difference to the all-Irish character of Ireland's international cricketing selections. Although club competitions are organised at provincial and district levels, the international eleven is chosen from players throughout Ireland and, in addition, a knock-out competition is contested by clubs from both parts of Ireland each season. Although international fixtures against Scotland, Wales, visiting touring sides, English counties and so forth attract little attention, there is no doubt that people throughout Ireland, regardless of political or religious affiliation, would favour an Irish victory. None of this, however, is to suggest that the game of cricket plays a significant role in the formation of an all-Irish political consciousness which transcends religious and cultural differences. The game's origins in Ireland would, alone, militate against such an achievement.

According to Stanley Bergin and Derek Scott, 'to gain a true picture of the history of cricket in Ireland it is necessary to relate the game to the political and social life of the country in the 18th century' (Bergin and Scott, 1980: 508). In terms of politics, this meant British rule and, as Bergin and Scott point out, 'whatever cricket was played in Ireland was confined essentially to the military, the gentry and members of the viceregal or Chief Secretary's staff and household' (ibid.).

The first recorded cricket match in Ireland took place in 1792 in

Phoenix Park, Dublin – the Garrison defeating an All-Ireland selection by an innings and 94 runs to win the wager of 1,000 guineas. According to W. P. Hone, it is almost certain that the future Duke of Wellington represented the All-Ireland side on this momentous occasion (Hone, 1956: 3). The captain of the Garrison, Colonel Lennox, was one of the chief founders of the Marylebone Cricket Club (M.C.C.) and he helped to popularise cricket in Scotland and in various parts of England as well as in Ireland. In his political life, he was to become Viceroy of Ireland and a figure of hatred for the Catholic party (ibid.: 5). Ironically, his opposite number in the Phoenix Park match, Major Hobbart, was given the task in 1792 of steering the Catholic Relief Bill through the Irish Parliament, for which he received little admiration from nationalists, including Wolfe Tone who described Hobbart as 'a monkey' and 'a fluttering English jay' (ibid.). The top scorer in the All-Ireland side was Secretary Cooke, later to become one of the functionaries employed by Castlereagh and Fitzgibbon to bribe members of the Irish Parliament to vote for the Act of Union (ibid.).

It is evident, therefore, that from the very outset cricket in Ireland was bound up with the politics of the day and was intimately connected to the British presence in the country. With that in mind, it is rather curious to note that some of the earliest clubs to be established in Ireland, during the 1820s, were in Ballinasloe, Carlow and Kilkenny, all of which were to become strongholds of Gaelic games in the years that followed (Bergin and Scott, 1980: 508). On closer inspection, however, it becomes clear that the English influence was again crucial. As Hone surmises,

> it may be that boys coming home by coach and ship from their English schools lamented that their favourite games could not be enjoyed during their summer holidays and that their fox-hunting parents, themselves hard put to know how to pass the summer months, saw in cricket a means of gratifying their gregarious instincts. (Hone, 1956: 6)

As a result of similar influences, former pupils of the English public schools ensured that cricket was played at Dublin University from as early as 1827 and a club was formed there in 1842, approximately 10 years after the establishment of the Phoenix club with its strong military connections.

Ironically, in view of the subsequent development of Ireland's constitutional history, cricket took hold more quickly in what was later to become the Irish Republic than in the north-east corner of the island. As Hone expresses it, 'no doubt the game was played in Ulster almost as early as in the South, but it seems to have been of slower growth' (ibid.: 38). Lisburn Cricket Club was founded in 1836 but it was not until the 1860s that the game began to spread rapidly in Ulster, following the formation in November 1859 of the North of Ireland Cricket Club under the patronage of the Lord Lieutenant of Ireland and the visit to Belfast, in 1861, of an All-Ireland team led by Charles Lawrence, a professional player who had been engaged by the Phoenix Club. From then onwards, cricket made even greater progress in Ulster than in other parts of Ireland, not least because of the continued dependence elsewhere on participation by the military and the influence of the English public school system.

How then did Irish nationalists respond to the emergence and growth of the game of cricket? Some surprising facts are to be uncovered in the history of Irish cricket. For example, the game was introduced into Co. Wicklow by John Henry Parnell, father of the Nationalist leader Charles Stewart Parnell. According to Hone, 'the great Parnell . . . inherited his father's taste for the English game . . . and he captained the Wicklow team for many years before entering nationalist politics' (ibid.: 11). In one season, C. S. Parnell averaged 35 with the bat. This naturally involved Parnell in matches against members of the British administration and garrison. By a bitter twist of fate, however, after his adoption of the nationalist cause, his favourite game was to be affected adversely at his own hands and those of his followers inasmuch as the growth of the Land League and the resultant deterioration in relations between landlords and their tenants brought about the demise of most of the small cricket clubs which had been situated outside of Belfast, Dublin and the Anglo-Irish Pale (ibid.: 12–13).

Nevertheless, during the intervening period, a number of Catholic schools had taken up the game of cricket, among them Clongowes Wood where a game crudely resembling cricket was first played as early as 1820 and the game in its proper form had become well established by the 1870s. It was at Clongowes Wood that another future Irish Nationalist leader acquired a love of cricket:

> John Redmond and his brother Willie were at Clongowes in these years, and it is curious to find that he, like his predecessor in the leadership of the Nationalist Party, Parnell, was also a bit of a cricketer. (ibid.: 23)

One of Redmond's closest political allies, Tom Kettle, was yet another nationalist with a great affection for the sport (ibid.).

During the 1840s and 1850s the most prominent cricketing school in Ireland had been the Church of Ireland's St. Columba's. Even there, however, the game had flourished in a nationalist environment, albeit cultural rather than overtly political. The founder and headmaster of St. Columba's, the Reverend William Sewell, a Fellow of Exeter College, Oxford, was a cultural nationalist who ensured that the Irish language was taught in his school and who expressed concern that 'in the English

Public Schools to which the wealthier Irish Church people were already sending their sons, nothing would be taught of Irish Antiquity, and the boys would return to live their lives in Ireland as strangers to their country' (ibid.: 28). Clearly this concern did not lead Sewell to the conclusion that an appreciation of cricket was alien to Irishness.

The 1860s and 1870s witnessed the rapid growth of cricket in Ireland but this trend was halted to some extent, at least outside Ulster, both as an indirect consequence of Land League activities and as a direct result of the emergence of the G.A.A. with its avowed policy to usurp such 'foreign' games as cricket. It should not go unnoticed, however, that many of those who supported the G.A.A., and some of those who were active in its foundation, had learned an appreciation of organised sports through participation in British games like cricket.

Nevertheless, it is no accident that from the turn of the century onwards, cricket has been disproportionately more popular in Ulster, along with the Dublin area, than elsewhere in Ireland – that is to say, in those regions where anglophile sympathies were sufficiently strong to withstand the nationalist onslaught. To this day, cricket is played in the Irish Republic in only 3 per cent of vocational schools (the overwhelming majority of schools) and 25 per cent of fee-paying private schools (*The Irish Times*, 14 June 1990), underlining the fact that cricket in the Republic is, essentially, a middle-class sport. One strange anomaly, however, is the fact that it was only after the partition of Ireland that cricket became properly organised on an island-wide basis. The Irish Cricket Union came into existence in 1923 after a meeting between representatives of the Leinster Union and the Ulster Union in July of that year. The existence of the I.C.U. further facilitated contacts between cricketers from throughout Ireland and the relationships between cricketers from the Irish Republic and Northern Ireland have remained strong and friendly regardless of the vicissitudes in Ireland's political life, particularly since the onset of the Troubles. That cricket does have a quasi-political image, nevertheless, is best seen if one considers the character of the sport in contemporary Northern Ireland. Who plays cricket and what is the game's function in Northern Irish political culture?

Presently, it is convenient to employ four categories in order to classify Northern Irish cricket clubs. First, there are the old boys' clubs, traditionally linked with certain schools, notably in Belfast. Second, there are clubs specifically tied to particular institutions such as the Royal Ulster Constabulary, the Civil Service or the universities. Third, there are the clubs which serve the major urban areas of the Province. And, finally, there are numerous clubs scattered throughout Northern Ireland serving villages, small towns or particular districts of the larger towns and cities. Other categories of clubs did exist such as those specifically associated with landlords, parks departments and factories, but these have either disappeared or been subsumed within the structure outlined above. Also vanished from the Ulster scene are the large number of military cricket clubs which were influential in the game's early development, but which, for security reasons, had to abandon a regular commitment to sporting engagements with external leagues and organisations. In addition, there is an administrative distinction, resulting in separate competitions, between the north-west of the Province and the remainder. It is immediately clear from the number of clubs and players that cricket is a popular sport (at least in terms of participation rather than spectating). However, a superficial appraisal of the widespread distribution of cricket clubs throughout Ulster should not be taken as evidence that the game is popular with both communities. On the contrary, the great majority of club members are Protestants and most of the clubs are located in predominantly Unionist areas, including those small towns and villages which are Protestant enclaves in largely nationalist regions such as west Tyrone and south Derry. Given the game's English heritage and its historical association with British rule, this should not come as any major surprise. However, in the light of the amicable relations between cricketers, north and south, it demands some investigation if only to discover whether or not cricket is a game which could ever serve an integrative function in Northern Ireland's recreational life.

Since cricket is not a spectator sport to any great extent in Ireland, clubs can easily avoid sectarian attachments. Furthermore, since the majority of Northern Irish cricketers possess a deep love for the game, only a small minority would regard religious affiliation as a cause for denial of club membership. So why do so few Catholics play?

The answer to this question must be sought in a number of different areas. First, there is the cultural symbolism of cricket. It came to Ireland as a British game and it has failed to become so universally played that its 'foreignness' can ever be forgotten. As a result, it is far easier for the spokesmen of Gaelic games to dissuade young men from playing cricket than to lure them from association football. A second factor, however, that is related in part, reveals why so few Catholics would opt for cricket even if it could be freed from its pro-British connotations. Cricket is seldom played in Northern Ireland's Catholic schools or colleges. Football, on the other hand, is played in an even higher proportion of Catholic grammar schools than Protestant ones. The results are there for all to see. A third and final factor is the location of cricket clubs, particularly the smaller ones. A great many grew up in communities which were, and have remained, almost exclusively Protestant, being sponsored by local aristocrats and factory and mill owners, who were either English by birth or educated in England. Thus, a tradition of playing cricket was established which has persisted to the present day. In these communities it is doubtful if Catholic incomers would be actively encouraged or would show any inclination to join the local cricket club.

On the basis of the foregoing analysis and in spite of the all-Ireland identity of cricket and the camaraderie which abounds, it is unlikely that cricket could ever play a part in helping in the process of integration through sport. On the contrary, because of its anglophile connotations, cricket has already been a casualty of sectarian politics in Northern Ireland. Cliftonville Cricket Club was burned out of its premises in north Belfast in 1972, two years after the club's centenary. Through the polarising demographic shifts which followed the serious rioting of the early 1970s, this area of north Belfast went from being neutral to being predominantly Catholic. The presence of one of the Province's oldest cricket clubs in the neighbourhood was unacceptable to local nationalists. According to its souvenir brochure (1990), Cliftonville Cricket Club 'fell victim to elements who were hostile to the club and what it represented in the area'. Cliftonville were forced to relocate in Greenisland, an area on the outskirts of the city which is largely Protestant. Ironically, because in certain Protestant circles the name Cliftonville suggested Catholic territory, a number of Greenisland loyalists mistakenly assumed that the cricket club was Catholic and anti-Catholic slogans were daubed on its new premises!

Even if more northern Catholics could be attracted to the sport, cricket's significance in Ireland's sporting life is scarcely large enough to allow it to make a major contribution to community reconciliation. Its major winter counterpart as a British game, however, is not only more popular, but has a higher public profile and is played by Irishmen at the highest international level. It is time now to examine whether the development of rugby union in Ireland mirrors the cultural isolation of cricket. Or does rugby serve an integrative purpose which cricket cannot do?

RUGBY UNION

Like cricket, rugby union is organised on an all-Ireland basis. There is an annual inter-provincial tournament contested by the four historic provinces. International selection is made from throughout Ireland. Although club competitions have been traditionally restricted to the two parts of Ireland, challenge games between clubs from the north and the south have guaranteed that contact, even between junior sides, is maintained. Furthermore, in season 1990–91, an All-Ireland League was introduced for the first time with room initially for only 19 of the 48 senior clubs in Ireland. (Nine in Division One and ten in Division Two.) After the first year of competition three clubs were relegated from

Division Two and only two promoted, thus reducing the number of elite clubs to 18. Entry to these new leagues and subsequent promotion and relegation were based on results in existing provincial league competitions. The main object of this exercise is to raise the standard of Irish rugby, but there is also a widespread feeling that it is logical to build upon the ties which already exist within the Irish rugby fraternity. The unification of Ireland may not be on the political agenda, but the implication is plain – Irish rugby men are big enough and sufficiently magnanimous to offer the hand of friendship to their fellow players, officials and 'alickadoes', regardless of religion or politics. The formation of an All-Ireland League, however, is by no means the first reason seized upon by the Irish rugby fraternity to indulge in mutual back-slapping, and their self-congratulations have certainly not fallen on deaf ears.

Commenting on the Irish international side, John Beattie, former Scottish international and British Lion, wrote that 'if truth be told the Irish team are the one outfit that could persuade me that sport and politics do not mix.' 'Ireland', claimed Beattie, 'are proof that sport can rise above religion and politics and assist in breaking down the barriers peacefully' (*Scotland on Sunday*, 4 February 1990). A large claim indeed, but one that is supported vehemently by the main historians of Irish rugby union. Thus, in the words of Sean Diffley, 'Irish rugby has been remarkably free of any serious row since 1879 – which is a tremendous tribute to officials and players' (Diffley, 1973: 14). Diffley accepts that 'the recent troubles in Northern Ireland created their own problems and it was not always easy to preserve the social and sporting *bonhomie* of rugby football', but adds that rugby has been 'disrupted much less than many would suppose' (ibid.). In similar vein, Edmund Van Esbeck comments that, despite the disruption caused by external events such as World Wars, the Easter Rising, the Civil War and the Troubles, 'the friendships and good fellowship of Irish rugby men were not affected by differing loyalties and political sympathies, and this great sporting bond continues to be a bright feature in the most gloomy times' (Van Esbeck, 1974: 90–91). Elsewhere Van Esbeck makes the point even more emphatically, arguing that rugby 'has succeeded admirably where successive generations of politicians have failed miserably', and that its success and the great development of the game in Ireland, notably in recent years, has been 'one of the most satisfactory sociological elements of Irish life' (Van Esbeck, 1986: 218). Diffley embellishes this point, stating that 'rugby-playing Irishmen are just as nationalist or unionist, or Protestant or Catholic as their non-rugby neighbours but they eschew all sectional labels when it comes to pulling on a rugby jersey' (Diffley, 1973: 14). Whereas politics have too often tended to divide the people of Ireland, 'rugby football has worked to widen friendships and unite' (ibid.). Thus, according to Diffley, 'what rugby football has done for

Ireland is to provide a different definition of Irishmen from the acrimonious, sterile political one' (ibid.). All of this is high praise and from impeccably well-informed sources. When politics do intrude into the world of Irish rugby, the causes are said to be factors extraneous to the game itself – problems relating to contact with South Africa, for example, or the refusal of certain international and club sides to travel to Ireland, north or south, when the Troubles have appeared to be passing through particularly sensitive stages. The game itself, however, is presented as wholly apolitical and the inference one might draw from the foregoing glowing reports is that a solution to the problems of Ireland could be found rather easily if all Irishmen took up the game of rugby football. The reality, however, is much less encouraging and one suspects that rugby's friends protest a little too much when their sport's capacity to unify is questioned.

To suggest that the history of rugby in Ireland is almost wholly free from controversy and to imply further that the sport has played a significant role in the transcendence of political and cultural differences are naive enterprises to say the very least. One need only examine, first, the development of Irish rugby and, second, the sport's contemporary character, particularly in Northern Ireland, to see that the game is deeply implicated in the cultural politics of division.

Like cricket, rugby arrived in Ireland as a direct result of British influence. There is a belief, which is particularly popular in Gaelic circles, that rugby is in fact a derivative of Cad, the ancient form of football played in Ireland. This is based on suggestions that as a youth, William Webb Ellis, the Rugby schoolboy who is reputed to have introduced the passing and carrying game into English public schools, spent his summers in County Tipperary in southern Ireland where his father, an officer in the British army, was stationed. It is argued that during these summer breaks Ellis was introduced to Cad by the locals and that he in turn introduced a form of Gaelic football to his friends during term-time at Rugby. However, given that Ellis's influence on the game of rugby in England is considered to have been slight by sports historians, it is very doubtful that Irish rugby owes anything to the rough and tumble of young William's holidays in Tipperary. Many of the earliest rugby games were in fact organised by cricket clubs. The oldest rugby club in Ireland is that of Trinity College, Dublin (T.C.D.), founded in 1854. Indeed, the only older club anywhere which remains in existence is Guy's Hospital. The founding members of the T.C.D. club included many who had been educated at Cheltenham and Rugby in England and the club's first Honorary Secretary/Treasurer was Robert Henry Scott, born in Dublin but himself a former pupil of Rugby School.

In Ulster the first rugby club to be formed was North, a rugby offshoot of the North of Ireland Cricket Club. The North Club was founded in 1865 and in the following year a rugby club was also established at Queen's University, Belfast (Q.U.B.). Rugby fixtures began to proliferate and in 1871–72 North played against teams from Dublin and Scotland as well as against Q.U.B. and the royal schools of Dungannon and Armagh. 1871 also witnessed the first match between North and Trinity, played at Ormeau in Belfast. By 1873–74, the game had taken hold in two of Belfast's major schools, the Royal Belfast Academical Institution and Methodist College, and from then to the present-day, schools rugby has been an important feature of Ulster's social as well as sporting life.

The first representative match played by Ireland took place on 15 February 1879 at the Kennington Oval in London, the opponents being England. According to Van Esbeck, 'the Irish team that played at Kennington was . . . the product of a co-operative venture between the north and south of Ireland' (Van Esbeck, 1974: 2). Indeed, Van Esbeck observes that there even existed at that time cordial relations between the rugby fraternity in Ireland and the protagonists of distinctive Gaelic games and pastimes (ibid.: 5–6). Two of the G.A.A.'s founders played rugby, George St J. McCarthy for Trinity College and Ireland and Michael Cusack himself, who went on to coach the game at both Blackrock College and his own Cusack's Academy.

None of this, however, should obscure the fact that the British influence was crucial in the introduction and subsequent reception of rugby in Ireland. Some nationalists *were* attracted to the game, but the vast majority were not and the development of rugby depended to a huge extent on the participation of Protestants or, at the very least, those who identified with the Union. This alone helped the G.A.A. considerably in its efforts to dissuade young Irishmen from engaging in a 'foreign' pastime. A number of Jesuit schools did adopt the game but this would have affected only a very small minority of the Catholic population, primarily members of the upper middle classes.

An early historian of Irish rugby suggested that the administration of the game in Ireland began with a split (McCarthy, 1892). On 14 December 1874, the Irish Football Union (I.F.U.) was established in Dublin and 13 January of the following year saw the formation in Belfast of the Northern Football Union of Ireland. Van Esbeck, however, denies that there was any split as such. 'Two unions there certainly were in the early days', he concedes, 'but a split there was not' (Van Esbeck, 1986: 21). Nevertheless, his explanation of why a separate union was formed in Belfast is scarcely convincing evidence of the absence of a split. He writes that 'the rugby fraternity in Belfast, and the North Club in particular, did not take kindly to Dublin running the show' (ibid.: 22). This point is endorsed by Diffley, who is less reluctant than Van Esbeck to use the actual word 'split' and who suggests that there was considerable anger in Belfast when the I.F.U. was formed in Dublin (Diffley, 1973: 12–14). It seems pointless to deny, in fact, that for the first five years rugby in Ireland was administered by two separate unions and that relations between the two were cool throughout the period.

On several occasions the I.F.U sought to open negotiations aimed at the creation of a single controlling body but their proposals did not find favour with the Northern body until 1880. Indeed, as Van Esbeck concedes, 'in the intervening period there were occasions when the prospect of the great union looked to be in great jeopardy' (Van Esbeck, 1986: 35–6). Two factors were primarily responsible for the eventual formation of a single Irish Rugby Football Union (I.R.F.U.), which met for the first time on 5 February 1880 and has remained in operation to the present day. The first was concern at Ireland's poor international performances which, it was felt, may have been attributable in part to the divided administrative process. The other factor was that in the preceding months Munster rugby officials had seemed intent on establishing their own union which would have resulted in even greater confusion than existed already. Thus, the split was brought to an end and, with Connaught joining the I.R.F.U. in 1885, rugby was united throughout Ireland under a single administrative body.

That problem negotiated, the historians of Irish rugby speedily return to their benign accounts of the game's development. As Diffley expresses it, for example,

> the split having been disposed of, Irish rugby has been almost as placid as a South Sea lagoon over the past 95 years. Wars and rumours of wars, social upheavals, the situation peculiar to Ireland of two political entities, none have made much dent in the united progress of rugby in Ireland. (Diffley, 1973: 14)

But is this description accurate?

In fact, the condition of rugby union in Ireland has never been as tranquil as Diffley and Van Esbeck suggest. Indeed their own accounts provide evidence to the contrary. It is true, of course, that rugby has not come to be regarded as an exclusive and politically charged sport comparable with those sponsored by the G.A.A. and nor has its development been as adversely affected as that of association football by the impact of Ireland's social and political divisions. But at no time has the game been wholly free from political controversy and rugby's role in helping to consolidate certain political and cultural attitudes should never be overlooked.

Despite the split which had preceded its formation, the new I.R.F.U. managed to progress in a highly successful manner into the twentieth century. The Great War interfered through the loss of life inflicted on players and officials and the disruption of fixtures. More serious, however, in terms of the public profile of Irish rugby were events leading up to the Easter Rising of 1916 and the subsequent developments in Irish politics. Again, the curious anomaly of Irish nationalists playing the British game can be discerned. The struggle for Irish independence was taken up by a number of rugby players, including Kevin Barry who had played for University College, Dublin, and the future leader of the Irish Free State, Eamon de Valera who had exhibited a preference for rugby as opposed to Gaelic games – a preference which was to become rather more muted after he had assumed the role of head of state (Van Esbeck, 1986: 82). However, it should be stressed that a majority of the rugby fraternity in Ireland opposed the nationalists at this stage. Among them was the President of the I.R.F.U., Frederick Browning, who, by a strange twist of fate, was killed when his Veterans' Corps Unit which had been on a route march on Easter Monday, 1916, was fired at by members of de Valera's garrison under the misapprehension that Browning's unit consisted of combat troops. As Van Esbeck expresses it, 'it was a sorrowful incident, and a grim quirk of history that the president of the union should have lost his life in a confrontation, however remote and undesigned, with another man who played and loved rugby football' (ibid.: 92). It was, in fact, a dramatic illustration of the extent to which politics intrudes on every aspect of life in Ireland. Rugby could not be an exception.

Meanwhile, in Northern Ireland the Protestant anti-Home Rule lobby developed a military dimension with the formation of the Ulster Volunteer Force (U.V.F.). As Williams (1989) discovered, Ulster's leading rugby club, North of Ireland, supported this development and in 1913 suggested that the second half of the rugby season should be cancelled. This was to encourage and enable rugby playing Protestants to join the U.V.F. and divert their energies away from sport towards the defence of the Union. The following season, North cancelled all of its fixtures and gave over its ground on the Ormeau Road in the centre of Belfast for the training and drilling of Protestant paramilitaries.

Such activities were bound to have a residual effect in rugby playing circles once partition had been established. As Diffley recognises, 'entrenched attitudes caused some problems for a while after the founding of the Irish Free State in 1922' (Diffley, 1973: 47). He records that there was, apparently, a reluctance at first in some quarters to fly the 'Irish tricolour (which, of course, had replaced the Union Jack as the national emblem) at Lansdowne Road for international matches' (ibid.). This problem had to be confronted by the I.R.F.U. which was now 'in the position of governing the game for one island which contained two separate political entities' (Van Esbeck, 1986: 97). According to Van Esbeck, 'the question was resolved in 1925 by the union designing a special flag of its own' (ibid.). However, as Van Esbeck himself admits, 'there were many who felt that when Ireland played at Lansdowne Road, she should do so under the national flag' (ibid.). Thus, contrary to his original statement, Van Esbeck indicates that the problem had not been fully resolved. Indeed, the request to fly the national flag continued to be made and provoked contrasting responses. It certainly did not meet with the approval of all the I.R.F.U. committee members and, as Van Esbeck concedes, this was 'perhaps an understandable position among a body of men who shared a common interest in rugby but whose political outlooks were diverse in the extreme' (ibid.).

The issue was raised again in January, 1932, by the Connaught branch of the I.R.F.U.. Again the Union insisted that its own flag would be flown at all international matches, regardless of whether these were played at Lansdowne Road, Dublin, or Belfast's venue for international rugby, Ravenhill (bought by the I.R.F.U. in 1923). But still the controversy would not go away. As Van Esbeck points out, 'the call for the flying of the national flag was taken up by the press and by many of the clubs' (Van Esbeck, 1986: 98). Foremost among the clubs engaged in the agitation was University College Dublin. In addition, the controversy developed into a fully fledged political issue to be pursued at the highest governmental level, when the Minister of External Affairs of the Irish Free State requested a meeting with the president of the I.R.F.U. to discuss the matter (ibid.).

According to Van Esbeck, this meeting brought a satisfactory resolution of the problem. 'That meeting', he writes, 'resulted in the union, without a dissenting voice, deciding on 5 February 1932 that in future the national flag would be flown alongside the union flag at all international matches at Lansdowne Road' (ibid.). That this decision did not, and could not, extend to cover matches at Ravenhill is worthy of note given the later course of events. Van Esbeck, however, as on the issue of the origins of the I.R.F.U., is quick to bring to a close discussion of a problem which had been potentially divisive. Thus, he concludes that 'an issue that had initially raised the passions of many inside and outside the game was resolved yet again with the fine balance that has maintained the unity of purpose within the game in Ireland, even if that balance has not been matched in the political arena' (ibid.).

It is undeniable that the I.R.F.U. has been assiduous in its efforts to avoid political controversy. Diffley, indeed, describes the Union's attitude as 'almost paranoiac' (Diffley, 1973: 46). The result has been a climate of secrecy such that issues of a controversial nature often do not come to light until events themselves have moved on. This should not lead one to suppose, however, that the issues were unimportant and could now be safely forgotten.

Apart from the flag issue, the inter-war period also witnessed controversy surrounding the question of whether or not rugby games should be played on Sundays. Raised in any sporting context, this question has tended to highlight a fundamental difference of attitude between Catholics and Protestants. Thus, today in the Irish Republic major sports are played widely on Sundays whereas in Northern Ireland only Gaelic games are played at a serious competitive level on 'the Sabbath'. The issue of Sunday rugby first emerged in the early 1930s. It was used, in fact, by some members of the Leinster Branch to oust certain members of the I.R.F.U. committee (Diffley, 1973: 47). To this day, however, the vast majority of rugby matches played in Ireland, and nearly all of those involving northern clubs even when in opposition to rivals from the Irish Republic, take place on Saturdays or on weekdays.

The next major controversy to affect Irish rugby took place in 1954 and showed clearly that the question of flags and emblems had not been successfully resolved, despite Van Esbeck's claims. In fact, Van Esbeck ignores the events of 1954 and it is Diffley who informs us that on the eve of an international match to be played in Belfast between Ireland and Scotland, southern members of the Irish side threatened strike action if certain grievances were not addressed. Diffley explains that:

> . . . this was a time of rather simplistic attitudes in Irish politics and some of the southern players held a meeting on the morning of the match and decided that they were not prepared to stand to attention before the game for the British national anthem unless the Irish anthem was also played and the Irish tricolour flown, both of which were illegal north of the border. (Diffley, 1973: 49)

Although Diffley describes the attitudes involved as 'simplistic', the importance of symbolism in Irish politics and thus flags and emblems should never be underestimated. Indeed, the Flags and Emblems Act which had outlawed the Irish tricolour in Northern Ireland was the subject of considerable deliberation by the members of the All-Ireland Forum and those who later formulated the Anglo-Irish Agreement. One of the first outcomes of these negotiations was the repeal in 1987 of the Flags and Emblems Act. In 1954, however, the problem created by the southern-based rugby internationalists was resolved, not by legislation but by way of a compromise arrived at by a southern I.R.F.U. committee member and the players involved who agreed to go ahead with the game, and the preceding formalities, in exchange for a promise that they would never again be expected to play international matches in Belfast. In fact, all future Irish International rugby games were to be played in Dublin under the Tricolour and preceded by the Soldier's Song, the Irish national anthem, ensuring that the sensitivities of Irish nationalists would not be offended. In due course it became apparent that the decision to play all games in Dublin would have been taken regardless of the political protest, for the simple reason that the Lansdowne Road ground was larger than Ravenhill and, thus, greater gate receipts could be generated if all matches were played there. It should be noted, however, that for the 1987 Rugby World Cup in the Antipodes, the I.R.F.U took the curious decision to drop the Soldier's Song and use the Londonderry Air (Danny Boy) as the Irish team's theme song. Traditionally, the unofficial anthem of Northern Ireland, the Londonderry Air, has been used by the Northern Ireland team in the Commonwealth Games. The fact that for the Rugby World Cup it was used instead of the Irish anthem can only be explained in terms of the powerful influence of the Ulster lobby within the I.R.F.U..

This decision was reversed for the 1991 World Cup and, once again, the playing of the Soldier's Song preceded Ireland's matches. It is significant, however, that the only players who sang the Irish national anthem were the minority of players who were indigenous to the Republic of Ireland. Players from Ulster and those whose Irish eligibility was vested in relatives either did not know the words to the national anthem or did not choose to sing them.

To explain the attitude of northern Protestants to the current state of affairs in Irish rugby, it is necessary to make a distinction between the views of members of the rugby fraternity and those of the wider public. The majority of the latter take an interest in Irish rugby only on the occasion of major international matches and, for the most part, hope for Irish victories regardless of the composition of the national side and the fact that its home games continue to be played exclusively in the Irish Republic surrounded by symbols of Irish nationalism. It should be added, however, by way of qualification, that doubts are frequently expressed concerning the international selection process, with northerners expressing fears that even in seasons when Ulster has been the most successful provincial side this fact will not necessarily be reflected in the composition of the international side and the sensibilities of the other provinces will be taken into account. Doubts of this type were raised concerning the events which surrounded the removal in season 1989–90 of Ulstermen Willie Anderson from the Irish captaincy and subsequently Jimmy Davidson from the position of national coach. Since the deliberations of selection committees, in any sport, are always shrouded in secrecy, it is impossible to offer empirical evidence to support this northern cynicism. But instinctive emotion plays a potent role in Northern Ireland's politics, whatever the facts of any given situation, and the feeling that a prejudice against northern players exists is sufficient to lead many unionists to the conclusion that this all-Ireland side, despite its northern Protestant players, is not completely their own in the way that the Northern Ireland football side, regardless of its Catholic players, most definitely is.

The attitudes of the rugby fraternity clearly differ markedly from those of the public at large. Members of the Protestant community in Northern Ireland continue to play the game enthusiastically and they regard international selection as the supreme personal achievement, regardless of the fact that this involves playing in Dublin in a context which is characterised by Irish nationalist symbolism. How can this be explained? Furthermore, how is it that, in spite of tensions and the occasional controversy, the picture of peace and tranquility, so cherished by the historians of Irish rugby, can be maintained?

To answer these questions, a number of points must be made about contemporary rugby in Ireland, north and south. One should never forget that rugby came to Ireland as a direct result of British influence. Thus, when Protestants represent Ireland, even though the match is played in Ireland and they are outnumbered in the side by southern Catholics, nevertheless they are playing a game which owes its existence in Ireland to the past domination of that country by Britain and which has succeeded in coping with the challenge made by those who have argued that to play anything other than Gaelic games should be regarded as the act of a traitor. In this context, the anomaly is less that northern Protestants play rugby for Ireland than that southern Catholics are willing to represent their nation at a foreign game. There can only be two explanations for the latter.

The first is to be found in the social composition of the rugby fraternity in the Irish Republic. Some are Protestants. Most have attended private schools which, whether Catholic or Protestant, were modelled on those English insititutions in which the game of rugby football was first developed. Rugby is played in 63 per cent of such schools, whereas only 25 per cent of the Republic's private schools offer Gaelic games. A small minority of free secondary schools play rugby (9 per cent), indicating that the game has a solidly middle- to upper-class base in the Republic. A former player, refers to 'the narrow social base of the game in Ireland' (Mark Langhammer, 1989: 13). Indeed, the Limerick area of the Irish Republic, for example, is frequently singled out as an exception because of the wider social base upon which rugby rests there in contrast with other parts of Ireland. Thus, because of their social backgrounds, whether they come from the north or the south of Ireland, rugby players and administrators tend to be comfortable in a middle-class culture which is at least partially rooted in English traditions.

The second explanation for southern Catholic participation in a foreign sport paradoxically can be traced to a particular expression of Irish nationalism. By their very sporting preference, rugby men are obviously not Irish nationalists in the narrow sense which we have applied to those who choose to play Gaelic games. Certainly, few would regard the unification of Ireland by way of non-constitutional methods as desirable. Nevertheless, they are still patriots, and just as sportsmen in other former colonies strive for excellence in games brought to them by their former masters as a means of confirming national confidence, the Irish use rugby as an expression of their patriotism in much the same way.

The middle-class location of southern Irish rugby applies equally in Northern Ireland, but the character of its constituency is rendered more complex because of the stark sectarian divisions which exist there. Although some clubs in Northern Ireland, particularly those like Malone which lack obvious 'feeder' or 'nursery' schools, have made attempts to broaden their appeal both to members of the working class and Catholics, in general the rugby fraternity in Northern Ireland can be characterised as middle class and Protestant (ibid.). In fact, in terms of class, religion and world view, the rugby players and officials in Northern Ireland form what is perhaps the most cohesive group to be found anywhere in Irish sport. We should not assume, however, on the basis of their endorsement of all-Ireland rugby and their harmonious relations with their southern counterparts, that they are an apolitical or a liberalising influence in Northern Ireland, or a force for integration.

As regards political attitudes, the rugby men of Northern Ireland for the most part endorse the views of the social and cultural community from which nearly all of them originate. The Protestant middle classes have seldom been regarded as potent political agents during most of the Troubles in Northern Ireland. Indeed, the image has often been created that but for the intransigence of the working classes on both sides of the sectarian divide, particularly Loyalists, a way out of the current impasse would have been revealed some time ago. The implication is that middle-class Protestants are much less implacable in their opposition to political developments which might lead ultimately to some kind of all-Ireland settlement.

The only evidence which can be provided in support of this benign analysis, however, is of a superficial nature. Middle-class Ulster Protestants are more likely to have direct contact with the Irish Republic. They are less likely to man the barricades during times of crisis. And, of course, given the preceding discussion, unlike association footballers, the rugby players among them are perfectly happy to play for an all-Ireland team and support cross-border links with enthusiasm. This 'evidence', however, is insubstantial when one considers the political realities. For all these contacts, middle-class Protestants in Northern Ireland have continued to vote in huge numbers for Unionism (whether in the form provided by the main Unionist parties or that of Alliance, or indeed most recently the newly formed Conservative Party branches in Northern Ireland). This is as much the case with rugby players as the other members of their community, who therefore live out a type of

Jekyll and Hyde existence. They play with and against players from the Irish Republic. At international level they stand to attention for the Irish national anthem and take as much satisfaction from beating England as do their southern team-mates. But in a game within a game, the Ulster representatives are particularly proud if the victory can be seen to have been secured more through their efforts than those of the players from the Republic. In political terms they have no desire to see a united Ireland and, perhaps partly as a subconscious reflection of that, they do little to encourage cross-community interest in Northern Irish rugby.

HOCKEY

In many ways the submerged political currents which play beneath the surface of rugby are more clearly visible in the world of Irish hockey. The roots of hockey in Ireland are virtually indistinguishible from those of cricket and rugby. Indeed, the three sports are often found co-existing in the same clubs. As a game involving stick and ball hockey can be viewed as the English alternative to the native Irish sport of hurling, and as one of a range of anglophile recreations which were competing with traditional forms of Gaelic sport in the later half of the nineteenth century (Dagg, 1944). The men's Irish Hockey Union (I.H.U.) was established in Dublin in 1893 and this was followed shortly by the establishment of the Irish Ladies' Hockey Union (I.L.H.U.). Indicative of the sport's heritage, the first men's president was the Reverend Canon Gibson, the headmaster of Kings Hospital Public School. Soon afterwards, the Provinces of Leinster, Munster and Ulster set up their own regional governing bodies, meaning that the Union was in fact a federation with each Province being partially autonomous. However, the strongholds of hockey, and the main Provincial rivals, were in the east and north of Ireland – in Leinster, the centre of British administration and influence at that time, and in Ulster, the heartland of Protestantism and Unionism. Illustrative of the demography of British influence in Ireland, Connaught, the island's most westerly Province, did not embrace hockey, preferring instead to concentrate on the Gaelic games of hurling and camogie. Even today, Connaught does not participate in senior inter-Provincial hockey.

Like rugby, hockey operates both within and between Provinces, and Ireland is represented in the sport by players drawn from both sides of the border. In this sense, hockey can be described as an all-Ireland sport. In order to avoid political problems, traditionally, when the all-Ireland team play they do so under the flag of the I.H.U., which consists of the crests of all four Provinces, in preference to the Irish Tricolour. Furthermore, players and officials stand to the Londonderry Air at the start of internationals, rather than to the Soldier's Song. However, relationships are not always so harmonious and neither are resolutions always so pragmatic.

Unlike the situation in rugby, whereby players from Northern Ireland are classified as Irish and can only play for the Irish national rugby team, to date hockey players have been able to play either for Ireland or Great Britain, or indeed, in the case of the men's game, both. This tradition of dual nationality has led to serious controversy in ladies' hockey and is beginning to have an impact upon the administration of the men's game. In 1980, two of Ulster's top senior ladies were banned from playing hockey for six years by the I.L.H.U. because, after being selected to play both for Great Britain and Ireland, Jenny Redpath and Violet McBride elected to play for the former. The case of Redpath was particularly controversial as, at the time the ban was imposed, she was captain of the Irish team. For her, the decision to play for Great Britain was made for a combination of sporting and political reasons. The Great Britain team is of a much higher standard than the Irish and would be expected to achieve greater success on the international stage. Thus, in terms of her hockey career it was a sensible decision. In addition, however, despite being the captain of the Irish team, she felt more British than Irish and experienced a greater sense of national pride when playing for Great Britain. Likewise, in 1991 Ulster players Joanne Menown and Jackie Burns, who were established as members of the Irish ladies' hockey team, elected to play for Great Britain – a decision which upset many senior administrators in the I.L.H.U., particularly since Ireland were drawn to play against Great Britain in the Olympic qualifying tournament.

This situation has been paralleled by events taking place within the men's game. Up until 1990, unlike the ladies' team, the all-Ireland men's team had never competed for a place in the Olympic games, places for which were by invitation only. Furthermore, the Great Britain men's hockey team was only constituted every four years in order to take up the challenge of participation in the Olympic Games. The rest of the time, as with rugby union, England, Scotland, Wales and Ireland have fielded individual teams and, in the absence of a Northern Ireland team, the best Ulster players have played for Ireland. However, rule changes within the International Olympic Committee (I.O.C.) meant that for the 1992 Games in Barcelona, the tradition of 'invite only' was abandoned in favour of holding a qualifying tournament. Ireland's participation in this qualifying tournament could have had two political side-effects. In the first place, the rules of the I.O.C. state that participating countries must march in the opening ceremony under their respective national flags and, if they win a medal, that flag should be raised at the medal ceremony and, in the case of the gold medal, accompanied by the corresponding national anthem. This means that in the unlikely event of the Irish winning a gold medal, the flag of the Irish Hockey Union and the Londonderry Air would have to be replaced by the Tricolour and the Soldier's Song. This scenario proved to be unacceptable to some of the game's senior administrators, particularly those from Ulster, who felt that it was disloyal to have a team which is comprised mostly of British citizens from Northern Ireland competing under the flag and anthem of the Irish Republic. Secondly, the Irish men's participation in the Olympic qualifying tournament meant that Northern Ireland's better male players would be confronted by the same difficult choice faced by Violet McBride and Jenny Redpath in 1980.

Stephen Martin is an Ulsterman who has won silver and gold Olympic medals with Great Britain's men's hockey team. Speaking on BBC Televison Northern Ireland's *Spotlight* programme, he revealed how complex the question of sports participation and national identity can be in the prevailing circumstances:

> It is a great honour to play for Ireland, but no-one ever feels that you are playing for your country as such because of the political situation here. When you play for Great Britain and Northern Ireland, as the team is described in the Olympic Games, then you feel you are playing for your country as such, but then it's one of those political dilemmas. (*Spotlight*, 1991)

The whole issue of whether or not to compete went to a vote, with Munster and Leinster voting in favour of entry, but with Ulster voting against, albeit by the narrowest of margins. However, the Ulster branch was bound by the majority decision and reluctantly agreed to bow to the Union's ruling, but not before the Chairman of the Irish selectors, Ulsterman Francis Baird, resigned in protest. The fact that Ireland subsequently failed to qualify for the Barcelona Olympics has done little to dampen passions within the I.H.U..

The fact that both Great Britain and Ireland continue to lay claim on the allegiances of hockey players from Northern Ireland means that the political dimension of sport in the Province has a more obvious impact on top hockey players than it does on their counterparts in other sports, such as association football and rugby. In the case of the latter, because Northern Ireland does not enter a separate team in the annual five nations championship series and because Ireland as a whole contributes players to the British Lions, questions of national identity are not usually raised when players from Northern Ireland are selected for either Ireland or the Lions; although in deference to sensitive issues of national sovereignty, in the Republic of Ireland there is a tendency among rugby pundits to refer to the latter as Great Britain and Ireland, rather than the British Lions. The situation in hockey is different and in many ways cameos the national question in general, particularly as it confronts Ulster Protestants. As we have seen, the written constitution of the Irish Republic effectively ignores the partition of 1921 by claiming statehood over the six counties of Northern Ireland which, since that time, have been part of the United Kingdom. Nevertheless, even though the people of Northern Ireland can legitimately claim to be British, because they are born in the island of Ireland, they have an equal claim to Irish citizenship. Not surprisingly, however, the majority of Ulster Protestants choose to consider themselves British rather than Irish, while many Catholics consider themselves to be Irish rather than British. This explains the logic of the arguments put forward by both Redpath and Martin. However, when British selection is not on offer and in the absence of a Northern Ireland hockey team, both players are willing and eager to play for Ireland, just like their counterparts in rugby. This reasoning involves a further consideration.

Notwithstanding relations with the Irish Republic, within the United Kingdom itself there is a high degree of national rivalry, particularly between England, the main political power, and the remaining countries of Scotland, Wales and Northern Ireland. Nowhere does this rivalry find clearer expression than in the world of sport, wherein beating the English generates great emotion and celebration among the non-English British. This is as true of the Northern Irish as it is of the Welsh and the Scots. As we shall see in the following chapter, the Province's soccer team provides a clearly defined outlet for the intra-United Kingdom nationalism of the Northern Irish. Alternatively, in sports for which the Province does not have national representative status, as is the case with rugby and hockey, most people in Northern Ireland are happy to play for and/or support an all-Ireland team, and this includes many Protestants and Unionists. However, for the latter, this display of cultural affiliation to Ireland does not translate into a political preference and is quickly abandoned in favour of patronage for combined United Kingdom teams and organisations when the level of sporting competition is raised to include Great Britain as an entity, as is the case with the Olympic Games. In this way, it can be argued that the Northern Irish Protestants are Irish in the same sense that the Welsh are Welsh and the Scots are Scottish: that is, at the level of culture they preserve a strong separate national identity while generally accepting the political authority of the British state. On the other hand, for many Northern Irish Catholics, sporting expressions of Irish nationalism are manifestations of a deeper seated feeling of fidelity to the Irish Republic and the desire for a united Ireland.

The middle-class values which surround the sports discussed in this chapter sustain the belief that sport and politics are separate spheres of social life and should remain as such. Nevertheless, as surely as the

G.A.A. provides a network for the development of nationalist sentiment in the Province, cricket, rugby and hockey clubs are part of the social fabric of Northern Irish Protestantism and as such have an important role in maintaining the status quo. In addition, throughout their histories all of these sports have been affected by the cultural and political divisions which have beset Ireland. In particular, the apolitical depiction of rugby offered by many of its spokespeople and leading commentators is appealing but essentially misleading. Rugby cannot be tarred with the same sectarian brush as Gaelic sport nor does it foster the deep-seated divisions which association football creates, but rugby flourishes in Ireland despite rather than because of the political attitudes of its administrators and practitioners. It is a largely middle-class game which, in Ulster, is played almost exclusively by Protestants, and to suppose that a sport which divides on horizontal and vertical lines can assist in creating better cross-community relations in Northern Ireland is a folly. Furthermore, as the situation in hockey clearly illustrates, changes in rules and regulations in the international arena can have the unintended consequence of further politicising sport in the Province. Should rugby ever become an Olympic sport and/or should Britain and Ireland compete against one another in the same competition, it is highly unlikely that Ulster's rugby fraternity would continue to prefer emerald green to red, white and blue.

4

WORLD SPORT IN AN IRISH SETTING

There are many other games played in Ireland which arrived as a result of the influence of the British, but which, unlike the sports examined in the previous chapter, have now become so universally popular that to be associated with them does not necessarily indicate a particular political preference or national affiliation. Individual sports such as tennis, trampoline, gymnastics, the martial arts and those activities associated with the wilderness have tended to avoid the worst excesses of political interference in Northern Ireland. Nevertheless, this does not mean that other world sports are always apolitical. On the contrary, the fact that many world sports are played and watched by large sections of both communities makes them vulnerable to political exploitation and sectarian practices. In this chapter we focus in some detail on association football, arguably *the* world game, to illustrate this point. Before doing so, however, we take a brief look at two other world sports, cycling and golf, to show how lower profile and essentially non-team games can likewise become engaged in the politics of division in Northern Ireland.

CYCLING

Cycling enjoys a huge following throughout Ireland, but as an organised competitive sport it has been unable to avoid becoming entangled in sectarian politics. Once more, the main issue for competitive cyclists in Ireland revolves around national affiliation. In the early 1980s the world governing body, the Union of International Cyclists (U.I.C.), introduced legislation whereby member countries could only be represented through a single national association. This immediately rekindled a long-standing political dispute within the sport's governing body in Northern Ireland, the Northern Irish Cycling Federation (N.I.C.F.), which had strong links with both the Irish and the British cycling federations.

Ever since its foundation at the beginning of the century, there have been elements within the N.I.C.F. who have been vehemently opposed to the notion of a single, all-Ireland governing body. In the first place the N.I.C.F. developed under the rubric of the British Cycling Federation (B.C.F.), an arrangement which suited the loyalist sympathies of many of the organisation's Protestant members. Secondly, the first all-Ireland cycling body to emerge, the National Cycling and Athletics Federation (N.C.A.F.) developed within the embrace of the G.A.A. (Griffin, 1990). The nationalist overtones of the G.A.A. ensured the alienation of Ulster's Protestant cyclists, particularly during the years leading up to and immediately following partition. Competitive cycling in Ireland during the inter-war years suffered because of a series of official and unofficial disputes between the two rival governing bodies. A compromise was reached in 1949 whereby the Federation of Irish Cyclists (F.I.C.) and the N.I.C.F. adopted joint powers and responsibilities for cycling in the Irish Republic and Northern Ireland. However, this was never a harmonious relationship and the sport was riven with political controversy throughout the 1950s and 1960s, both at home in Ireland and overseas. Rival factions scuffled during races and equipment was sabotaged. In 1955 the start of the World Amateur Cycling Championships in Rome was delayed because two teams turned up to represent Ireland. Jointly licensed by the F.I.C. and the N.I.C.F., an official Irish team lined up alongside an unofficial, pro-nationalist team. The latter refused to withdraw and, in order to start the race, the organisers were forced to let down the tyres of the unofficial team.

As is the case with hockey, the change in international rules has resurrected the issue of national affiliation and has led to a split within the ranks of the N.I.C.F.. In the late 1970s a working party called the Irish Tripartite Cycling Committee was formed in an attempt to resolve the sport's organisational crisis. The group recommended that a unified Irish cycling federation should be formed, but this was rejected by the majority of the Protestant membership of the N.I.C.F.. After a high court battle, a splinter group, representing nationalist interests and affiliated to the Dublin-based all-Ireland body, broke away from the N.I.C.F. and formed the Ulster Cycling Federation (U.C.F.). In an attempt to resolve their differences, the N.I.C.F. and the U.C.F. brought in George Glasgow, the former Director of the Northern Ireland Sports Council, as a mediator, but despite his considerable skills as a diplomat, he was unable to craft an agreement between the two sides. Speaking on

B.B.C. Television Northern Ireland's *Spotlight* programme in 1991, Glasgow confessed that while he had solved a multitude of sporting problems he would never be able to solve Northern Ireland's cyclists' conflict so long as it remained bound up with Ireland's political crisis.

GOLF

Despite suggestions that golf may have enjoyed an early Celtic existence in Ireland (Browning, 1955: 7), it is generally accepted that, in its modern form, golf's ancestry should be traced to the Hamilton and Montgomery Plantation of Ulster in 1606 (Gibson, 1988: 1–7). According to one historian of the game, 'modern golf in Ireland is generally accepted as beginning with the founding of Royal Belfast Golf Club by a Scottish golfer, Mr George Baillie, in 1881' (Browning, 1955: 157). It is noted, however, that 'even before the establishment of the Royal Belfast Club, the game had been played at the Curragh, chiefly by the officers of Scottish regiments quartered there, and the Royal Curragh Club has a vague claim to existence dating from immediately after the Crimean War' (ibid.). Notwithstanding these important non-Irish influences on its emergence, golf in Ireland is now recognised as an international pastime and few nationalists would denounce it as a foreign game. Nevertheless, golf clubs traditionally have mechanisms which guarantee inclusion and exclusion and, at least in Northern Ireland, club membership can be used as a covert way of maintaining communal division. However, the fact that it is essentially an individual pursuit has tended to minimise the dangers of serious sectarian contamination. Some of its practitioners might even argue that it is a game for 'gentlemen' and 'ladies', and as such has no room for the worst excesses of Irish political life. Nevertheless, because golf clubs tend to be socialising centres for many of Northern Ireland's senior business and administrative executives, including security personnel, they have been regularly targeted by terrorists as sites for bombings and assassinations.

ASSOCIATION FOOTBALL

As is the case with cycling, the affairs of association football have been inextricably linked with politics throughout the past 100 years and are likely to remain so for the foreseeable future. In part, of course, this is the story of how political events intrude upon the ordinary life of football just as they do in other sports. Because of civil unrest, the Northern Ireland international team had to play a total of 10 'home' fixtures between 1972 and 1978 at grounds on the British mainland. In addition,

Irish League representatives withdrew from European competitions in season 1972–73 because of inter-community tension. Thus, the troubled political condition of Northern Ireland has had a damaging effect on the organisation of senior football. However, the linkage of association football and politics in Northern Ireland goes far beyond the direct impact of the troubles and resultant security considerations. The sport is played by members of both the Protestant and Catholic communities, frequently together or, at the very least, in direct competition, and would appear to offer a significant channel for reconciliation. In truth, however, the sport's capacity to divide has been at least as marked during most of the twentieth century as have been its integrative capabilities. Football has not simply been on the receiving end of Ireland's troubled political history. It has often reflected the divisions which have helped to create political unrest and, on occasions, has even helped to exacerbate these divisions.

Ball games have been played in Ireland for centuries. The oldest of these, the game of Cad, which was popular among all Celtic peoples, is thought to have originated at least 1,000 years ago. It involved carrying and kicking a ball across open country and resembled closely the form of football which was banned in England in 1365. But although a sporting ban was introduced in Ireland in the same year by the Proclamation of the Statutes of Kilkenny, the sport to which the authorities had taken exception was hurling rather than football or Cad. This was because of the relative unpopularity of the latter in Ireland and the fact that it was simply not regarded as posing a threat to public order or the status quo. Indeed, football must have been regarded as relatively harmless even as late as 1527, when it was excluded from a ban on all games which were believed to divert people from archery practice. On this occasion, the proscribed sports included hurling and handball, but not 'the great foote ball' (Van Esbeck, 1986: 7–11). What is worthy of note here is that although football was still not regarded as harmful, it was now accorded the status of an increasingly popular pastime among the Irish. Indeed, records exist of important seventeenth-century football matches held in the Slain area of County Meath and at Fingal near Dublin (ibid.: 7). Carrying the ball, however, remained an essential feature of these games.

By the eighteenth century football had become even more popular and, although frowned upon by members of the aristocracy, was played regularly at College Park in Dublin by students of Trinity College. The form of football played was still the carrying game but during the nineteenth century this was replaced in numerous English public schools by a kicking game. This latter form was brought back to Ireland by Irish pupils at these schools, either during vacations or on the completion of their studies. The rules of association football were formulated in England in 1867 by the Football Association and football was first played according to these rules in Ireland in 1885. The last recorded game of Cad took place in 1888 between the parishes of Cordal and Scartaglen. Henceforward, although handling was to be a major characteristic of both the Gaelic and rugby codes of football, the kicking game was established as one of Ireland's main sports.

That association football became a major Irish sport, however, is not to suggest that it was received with equal enthusiasm throughout the country and by all its people. Football in some form or another was established as an integral part of Irish sporting tradition, but the emergence of the specific association code owed more to non-native influences. In the southern part of Ireland these were felt most strongly in Dublin and its environs, where the Anglo-Irish tradition was most firmly established. This had the effect of making association football, to begin with at least, the preserve of a relatively small, middle-class section of southern Irish society. In the north east of Ireland, on the other hand, the sport was taken up almost immediately by a much larger section of the population. There are three main reasons for this. First, the north east was predominantly Protestant, a majority of its population the ancestors of the original Protestant settlers. Their receptiveness to non-Irish influences was thus greater even than that of the Anglo-Irish community in Dublin. Second, Northern Ireland's close links with mainland Scotland meant that the rapid advances made there in the growth of football had an immediate and direct influence on the introduction of the game in the Province. Thirdly, the Belfast area was the most industrialised region in Ireland at the end of the nineteenth century at a time when it was becoming apparent that the real strength of association football was to lie not in its popularity in the great public schools, but in its growth in the industrial regions of Britain. So Ulster's largely Protestant industrial communities provided the ideal conditions for the rapid development of the sport in Ireland, and to this day the Province's leading clubs are still important focal points of working-class culture.

The Irish Football Association (I.F.A.) was formed in Belfast in 1880, five years before the code was played officially in Dublin. The Irish Cup competition was instituted by the I.F.A. and first competed for in 1881. To underline the importance of British influence in disseminating the sport in Ireland, early finalists in the competition included soldiers of the Black Watch regiment and the Gordon Highlanders. In addition, leading Scottish and English teams made guest appearances in Belfast and surrounding areas as gradually the standard of play in domestic circles improved.

To begin with the I.F.A. assumed responsibility for administering association football throughout Ireland and sides from outside the Belfast area competed for the Irish Cup. However, it was not until 1906 that a Dublin side, Shelbourne, actually won the trophy and Shelbourne (1906, 1911 and 1920) and another Dublin club, Bohemians (1908), are the only teams to have taken the Irish Cup out of Ulster.

A similar picture emerges when one turns to the Irish League Championship organised by the Belfast-based Irish League authorities and first contested in season 1890–91. No club from outside Ulster has ever won the competition, the history of which has been dominated by Belfast teams. In fact, it was as recently as 1952 that the championship was taken out of the city for the first time, the victors being Glenavon from Lurgan in Co. Armagh. Again to emphasise the British links, early competitors included the North Staffordshire Regiment, the Scottish Borderers and the Royal Scots, who withdrew after only seven matches in season 1899–1900 on account of the outbreak of the Boer War and an entirely different challenge in South Africa.

Despite the relative lack of success on the part of Dublin clubs, the game of association football continued to grow in popularity in that city and elsewhere in Ireland. Athlone Town was formed in 1892, earlier even than Shelbourne (1895) and Shamrock Rovers (1899), and the Sligo Rovers Club was established in 1908. Regardless of the game's growing appeal, however, it remained closely linked with the Anglo-Irish community in Ireland, as well as with members of the army garrisons and the British administration. As such it was portrayed with some success by nationalists as a foreign game, incompatible with the pursuit of native Gaelic pastimes. This in itself was unlikely to prevent the further growth of the sport even in the most distant parts of the country. At that point, however, politics intervened overtly for the first time in the development of association football in Ireland and the game's various responses themselves took on a political character.

As the issue of Irish independence began to gather momentum, it became increasingly difficult to preserve the unity of football in Ireland. Shelbourne refused to play an Irish Cup semi-final replay at Windsor Park in Belfast in 1919 and further disputes resulted in Dublin clubs withdrawing from the Irish League. As Malcolm Brodie observes, 'unanimity no longer existed in Irish football. Hardline attitudes had developed between Belfast and Dublin. The split, admittedly minimal now, was soon to widen to a chasm' (Brodie, 1980: 15).

Finally, the creation of an Irish Free State, from which six counties of Ulster were excluded, prompted the Leinster Football Association to break from its parent body, the I.F.A.. Immediately, as Malcolm Brodie reports, 'Eire newspaper advertisements described matches in Dublin as being under the "Football League of Ireland" while games in Belfast were merely "Belfast and District"' (ibid.). Henceforward association football was to be organised separately in the different states of Ireland, with the Irish League and the Irish Football Association continuing to preside over the game's affairs on the northern side of the border, and the League of Ireland and the Football Association of Ireland (F.A.I.) assuming control in the south.

The impact of political and cultural division was now more overt than had been the case before partition. These political implications can be discerned in two distinct but related areas: first, the nature of football relations between Northern Ireland and the Irish Republic; and second, the football relations between the vying communities within Northern Ireland.

On the international front, the politics of football operate at two levels. On the one hand there are the attitudes of football administrators in Ireland, and on the other, there are the perceptions and behaviour of football supporters. Of the former it can be said that relations between administrators on different sides of the border have been, for the most part, far more amicable than those which have existed between their political counterparts. Nevertheless, the existence of two separate administrations on the same island, the political identity of which is contested, has created unavoidable difficulties. In 1954, these reached a peak when at the annual congress of the international football federation (F.I.F.A.), the F.A.I. proposed that only teams playing under its control should be described as Ireland. At that time, and indeed into the 1960s, the I.F.A continued to describe its representative sides as Ireland, the title of Northern Ireland becoming common only in the 1970s. This was resented by Dublin-based officials. Yet it should be remembered that long after partition, the I.F.A. continued to select its international sides on an all-Ireland basis and this situation did not change until 1950, the last all-Ireland selection being made in that year for the game against Wales at Wrexham. Furthermore, despite the tacit admission by the I.F.A. that it now lacked any authority over Irish football outside Northern Ireland, there was no likelihood that it would forfeit the right to be seen as representing Ireland. With the support of the other home unions, therefore, the I.F.A. sought to resist the F.A.I.'s challenge and the 1954 proposal was defeated. Thus, we have the strange situation of two Irelands competing in major international football competitions: a source of some terminological confusion to radio and television commentators.

The fact that the two sets of administrators are now able to coexist peacefully is the result of a realistic appraisal of the context in which they find themselves. First, given the political impasse which now exists, it is likely that the two separate political entities in Ireland will remain as they are for the foreseeable future. Separate governing bodies for the game of football are a straightforward acknowledgement of that fact. Second, given the relatively small size of Ireland's population, the situation which prevails allows for a larger number of football administrators per head of the population than would normally be the case. Thus, the sports administrators may have a vested interest in a pragmatic acceptance of the existing state of affairs.

These factors should be borne in mind when one considers the widespread resistance to the idea of an all-Ireland football team or the concept of an all-Ireland League competition. The other decisive factor however is the response of football supporters, particularly in Northern Ireland, to proposals of this nature.

Since the late 1970s, Northern Ireland and the Irish Republic have played four full international matches (in 1978 and 1989 in Dublin, and in 1979 and in 1988 in Belfast). Thanks in part to major security operations and restrictions on away supporters, these games passed off with a minimum of crowd disturbance. That is not to deny, however, the intense rivalry generated by these occasions. For many supporters the confrontations were invested with a significance well in excess of that which is usually attached to international football games, even those between such long-standing rivals as Germany and France or Scotland and England. Here, for many, were the latest instalments in the unfolding story of tribal conflict between two warring communities. It is ironic in these circumstances that the composition of the two sides on view has tended to be at odds with the picture conjured up by such graphic imagery. With the appointment of Jack Charlton, a former English international player and holder of a World Cup winners' medal, in the 1980s the F.A.I. began to turn to players whose links with Ireland are through grandparents rather than parentage or place of birth. This has led to the selection by an English manager of international sides in which less than half of the players were born in Ireland or could be regarded as natural members of the Irish nationalist community. The I.F.A. has also selected players designated as Northern Irish despite having been born outside the Province, but, in general, this policy has been less strenuously followed than it has been by the F.A.I. – hence northern scorn at some of the latter's selections and the popular joke that the letters F.A.I. stand for 'Find Another Irishman'! Nevertheless, Northern Ireland's team selections are themselves far less pristine than those who regard competition between the two Irelands as a re-enactment of old battles might wish to believe.

The I.F.A. has always selected Catholic players, not only while it reserved the right to select all-Ireland teams but even since its acceptance of a narrower field of influence. Some of these Catholic players, most notably Pat Jennings, Northern Ireland's most capped international player, attained legendary status in the eyes of Northern Ireland's supporters. Paradoxically, however, many of those who encouraged Jennings so vociferously were also likely to sing songs which directed abuse at the Catholic religion and to wave the colours red, white and blue to attest to their loyalty to the union. For many years this complex relationship was accepted as both unavoidable and, ultimately, harmless and it did little to deter Catholics from supporting the national team, which after all included members of their own community. Indeed, they could derive considerable amusement from hearing Protestant supporters break off from a chorus of 'The Sash My Father Wore' to sing the praises of big Pat from Newry or former Gaelic footballers, such as Gerry Armstrong and Martin O'Neill. This is a perfect illustration of the sanguine attitude towards sectarian abuse which most Northern Irish people have tended to adopt even during the lowest points in the current Troubles.

But the real tensions lie just below the surface and by the mid-1980s they had begun to make a serious impact on supporters' attitudes towards the Northern Irish team. Then, for the first time, substantial abuse was directed from the terraces towards Catholic players in the side, most notably Anton Rogan. In response, the I.F.A. took the unprecedented step of warning that the Spion Kop at Windsor Park, on which the most overt manifestations of loyalism had always been displayed, would be closed for future international matches if the practice continued. But why had it begun in the first place and what are its implications for support for the national team?

The reason why Rogan was singled out for abuse is that not only is he a Catholic from West Belfast, perceived in loyalist eyes as being almost entirely inhabited by republicans and fellow travellers, but he was chosen to represent Northern Ireland as a Glasgow Celtic player. The lingering influence of the Scottish game is highlighted by the widespread support in Northern Ireland for the major Glasgow teams which follows the same sectarian pattern as in Scotland itself. Given the enthusiasm of Northern Ireland Protestant football supporters for Celtic's traditional rivals, Glasgow Rangers, the presence of a Celtic player in the national squad naturally drew a less than enthusiastic response, which was soon transformed into outright hostility when Rogan made mistakes on the field of play. Indeed, another player similarly abused by supporters was Allan McKnight, himself a Protestant but also a Celtic player when first selected to play for Northern Ireland. However, by itself the Celtic connection fails to provide a full explanation for the increased hostility shown towards Catholic players in the 1980s, since in previous years Celtic players had been accepted by Northern Ireland supporters. Indeed, former Celtic players Bertie Peacock and Charlie Tully are remembered as two of the greatest and best loved players to have represented Northern Ireland in the post-war era.

A further explanation for the hostility shown towards Rogan is that it is the product of frustration on the part of the Northern Ireland followers. During the early 1980s the national side had enjoyed a period of unprecedented success, qualifying for the final stages of the World

Cup in both 1982 and 1986, and scoring notable victories against Spain in Seville (1–0, 25 June 1982) and West Germany in Belfast (1–0, 17 November 1982) and Hamburg (1–0, 16 November 1983). As experienced players retired and no immediate replacements were found, it became clear that the later years of the 1980s would be dedicated to team-building and little success could be anticipated. Exacerbating the problem, in the eyes of supporters, was the fact that the Republic of Ireland was enjoying international success for the first time, culminating in qualification for the final stages of the European Championships in 1988 and of the World Cup in 1990. For the first time it seemed as if the balance of football power in Ireland was shifting south. This realisa-tion was underlined when the Republic defeated Northern Ireland convin-cingly in Dublin on 11 October 1989 in the qualifying round of the European Championships.

Against this backdrop, criticism of Rogan and others can be seen as a response to what was regarded, in sectarian terms, as an enemy within. However illogical, particularly in the light of success enjoyed with Jenn-ings as the last line of defence, Northern Ireland's relative decline *vis-à-vis* the Irish Republic was attributed by some, many of whom would have found the concept difficult to articulate, to the presence of players in the team whose ultimate loyalty to Northern Ireland in general was questionable. This in turn raises broader political questions about the status accorded to the national football team in loyalist popular culture.

The third, and most serious, reason for the insults directed at Anton Rogan is that the nature of support for Northern Ireland has undergone a gradual transformation during the course of the Troubles. Central to unionist ideology is a sense of being under siege, heightened by the sign-ing of the Anglo-Irish Agreement which seemed to prove to many Protestants that their fears of being abandoned by Britain were well justified. As early as the late 1970s, in fact, the Ulster Defence Associa-tion (U.D.A.), together with some Unionist politicians, had come to accept that it might be necessary at some point for Northern Ireland to become independent in order to avoid the danger of incorporation into the Irish Republic. So many symbols of Protestant popular culture, however, are essentially British that the idea of independence demands for its acceptance a profound transformation in Protestant attitudes. In turn, this requires the existence of organisations and emblems which are exclusive to Northern Ireland and can sustain popular support for the demand for independence.

Few symbols were better equipped to serve this purpose than the Northern Ireland football team. It was living proof that Northern Ireland was and is a separate political entity, whatever politicians in Dublin and London might claim and nationalists in the Province might aspire to. During the 1980s, the red, white and blue scarves and Union Jacks were replaced on the terraces by the green and white colours, which the team had always worn, and Northern Ireland flags. Windsor Park, the national stadium but also home of Northern Ireland's most loyalist club side, Linfield, became an increasingly unfriendly place for Catholics – symbolised by the message 'Taigs Keep Out' daubed on a wall near one of the approach routes to the ground.

This issue was given added prominence at the beginning of 1992 when a local newspaper, the *Sunday Life* (5 January 1992), drew attention to comments made by Linfield manager, Eric Bowyer, in a Linfield fanzine. Bowyer made it clear that in the prevailing circumstances he could not envisage signing a Catholic player. Despite the policy reiterated by club secretary, Derek Brooks, not to 'exclude from its staff anyone by reason of colour, race or religion' (2 February 1992), Linfield came under attack from Father McManus, spokesman for the Irish National Caucus in the United States, who demanded that the I.F.A. sever its ties with Windsor Park and threatened to disrupt Northern Ireland's participation should they qualify for the 1994 World Cup finals in the United States. The secretary of the I.F.A., David Bowen, defended Linfield from the charge of sectarianism and pointed out that the I.F.A.'s relationship with Linfield is underpinned by a £3 million programme of ground improvements largely funded by the Government. Although Mr Bowen acknowledged that a boycott campaign would be embarrassing, he was confident that his organisation would receive full backing from F.I.F.A. (26 January 1992).

In March, however, after relentless lobbying by the Irish National Caucus, Coca Cola threatened to withdraw sponsorship from the I.F.A.. In addition, Thorn-E.M.I. ended their sponsorship of Linfield. While the company stated that this step was taken because of a down-turn in the economy, many believed that this was a result of the bad publicity which the club had received over the Bowyer affair. In the face of such pressures Linfield took the unprecedented step of holding a press conference at which they declared themselves to be a non-sectarian organisation, stating further that:

> People of all classes and creeds are welcomed at Windsor Park, both for Linfield games and for internationals, and the Management committee strongly refute the scurrilous and unfounded allegations made by Father McManus and his associates and their campaign to have commercial sponsorship withdrawn from soccer in Northern Ireland. (*Irish News*, 19 March 1992)

Club officials went on to detail the 70 Catholics who had played for the club since its inception in 1886. Close examination reveals that although many of these individuals played for the club in the post-war era, most did so in the period before the Troubles began in earnest in the late

1960s. Very few Catholics have played for Linfield since that time and they have all been recruited from outside of Northern Ireland. After considerable efforts, in the summer of 1992 they managed to sign one local Catholic. However, in the prevailing circumstances it is unlikely that Linfield's reputation as a Protestant symbol will be seriously challenged by this token gesture.

This does not present a problem for the majority of those who at present constitute Linfield's, and indeed Northern Ireland's, support. It is precisely because the Northern Ireland football team remains as one of the strongest reminders of the Province's separate political identity that Protestant supporters have remained loyal and regard Catholic shifts in allegiance as the latest example of the perfidy of the enemy within. Ironically, therefore, while the rising popularity of soccer in the Republic may have a progressive impact in terms of loosening the cultural stranglehold of the G.A.A., in Northern Ireland its effect has been to polarise the two communities further.

None of this is to suggest that a majority, or even a substantial minority, of Northern Ireland's supporters would favour independence as a solution to the present political crisis. What it highlights, however, is that under siege, people turn for solace to that which they can claim to be exclusively their own. The success of the Northern Ireland team was a source of comfort as well as of joy. When success receded into history, the enemy within would inevitably be the first to be singled out and blamed.

A survey carried out by McGivern in 1990 has demonstrated that affiliation to and support for national football teams by Northern Irish football supporters tends to reflect the complexity of the issue of religious/national identity in the Province. A hundred Catholic and a hundred Protestant football supporters from the greater Belfast area were invited to rank in order England, Northern Ireland, Wales, the Republic of Ireland and Scotland according to how they would prefer to see them finish in an international competition. Of the Catholics an over-whelming 91 per cent wanted the Republic of Ireland to come first. Only 8 per cent wished to see Northern Ireland win the competition, but 62 per cent hoped that they would come second behind the Republic. Of the Catholic sample, 64 per cent placed England in last place behind third-placed Scotland and fourth-placed Wales. On the other hand, 88 per cent of Protestants surveyed wished to see Northern Ireland victorious, followed by either Scotland (41 per cent) or England (39 per cent); 60 per cent placed the Republic of Ireland fourth or last. Significantly, how-ever, more than 40 per cent of the Protestant sample placed England lower than third place, with 24 per cent wishing to see them last behind Wales. In addition, in the event of the Northern Ireland national team being disbanded, respondents were asked to declare whether they favoured

Northern Irish players representing an all-Ireland or an all-U.K. team. Of the Catholics, 85 per cent favoured participation in an all-Ireland team. Protestant opinion was evenly divided, with 43 per cent preferring participation in an all-U.K. team and 42 per cent opting for an all-Ireland side.

These results confirm that Protestants clearly identify with Northern Ireland and have little regard for the team of the Republic, except perhaps when they are playing against England, as happened in the 1988 European Championships and the 1990 World Cup. The fact that many Northern Irish Protestants choose to support the Republic of Ireland over England cannot be taken as exemplifying a more general leaning towards Dublin. On the contrary, it illustrates the depth of mistrust generated within Northern Ireland's Protestant community by the many and varied attempts by successive English-dominated British governments to settle the 'Irish question' in Northern Ireland by admitting Dublin into the apparatus of political negotiation.

On the other hand, the majority of Catholics who follow football feel themselves to be best represented by the team of the Republic, and that furthermore they would prefer the Northern Irish team to be subsumed by an all-Ireland organisation. According to the author of the survey, these preferences are indicative of deeper seated political sentiments:

> The rejection of the Northern Ireland team and Windsor Park, which to Catholics symbolises Unionism in the form of the Union Jack flag, the British national anthem and the chanting of sectarian abuses probably conveys most Catholics' rejection of the Northern Ireland state. A state which they feel has nothing to offer them in terms of a history, a culture or an identity. (McGivern, 1991: 87)

At international level, therefore, many Catholics in Northern Ireland have turned their attention to the Irish Republic's team, partly no doubt because of the latter's recent achievements but at least as importantly because they feel that they are unwelcome intruders at Northern Ireland games. Yet, Catholics continue to play for the national side and, despite the rival attraction of Gaelic sport, they play an active role at all levels of the game within Northern Ireland. That they have done so since the arrival of the game in the Belfast area has not been without political implications, as can be seen when one examines the development of domestic league and cup football in Northern Ireland.

It is undeniable that as a game played by members of both communities, all age groups and, indeed, both sexes, football has an integrative potential in Northern Ireland. Catholics and Protestants play with and against each other on a regular basis and sectarian incidents are infrequent. In addition, the extent of interest in football is considerable in every corner of the Province, with many people supporting British clubs and investing time and money to watch their favourites. Although attachment to the Glasgow clubs follows sectarian lines, this is not the case as far as English sides are concerned, and as a result members of the rival communities are brought together by virtue of shared admiration for Everton, Liverpool, Leeds, Manchester United and the like. That said, however, the development of the domestic game has been influenced by political pressures and, despite its integrative potential, football has been a significant focus for sectarian rivalry and continues to perform that role in the present.

Although the arrival of association football in Northern Ireland was primarily due to British influences and Irish nationalists were quick to characterise the sport as foreign, Catholics in Northern Ireland were attracted immediately to the game. Initially, however, this enthusiasm was expressed at a personal level as no channel existed for a collective Catholic contribution to the game's development. Ironically, the body which filled that particular vacuum was to spring from a most unlikely source, namely that most anglophile of sports, cricket. In August 1891, a cricket team called the 'Sentinel' won a challenge match against the much vaunted opposition of 'Model Star'. After the game 'Sentinel' players, most of whom lived in the largely Catholic Falls area of Belfast, decided that there was so much sporting talent in the area that a football team should be formed. The outcome of their discussions was the establishment of Belfast Celtic.

The club was modelled, of course, on its illustrious Glasgow namesake which agreed to give its patronage to the newcomers and also sent a donation. The fraternal association between the two Celtics was to last throughout the history of the Belfast club (Kennedy, 1989: 3). In the eyes of Protestants, Belfast Celtic was already guilty by association; it was a nationalist side for nationalist players and supporters.

Contrary to the Protestant view, Belfast Celtic officials never regarded the club as an exclusively Catholic preserve and many of their most famous players were Protestants. In a society where myth is often more potent than fact, however, the popular image of Celtic was kept alive by friend and foe alike.

Belfast Celtic competed for the Irish League Championship for the first time in season 1896–97. From then onwards, games featuring the club and rivals Linfield and Glentoran, both supported for the most part by Protestants, were frequently marred by crowd disturbances.

In the second game of the 1896–97 season, Celtic's first in senior football, police had to separate rival factions during a match with Glentoran. Later that season, Linfield supporters attacked a Celtic player, Terry Devlin, during a game between the two sides. In the 1898–99 season, Celtic reached the semi-final of the Irish Cup to meet Glentoran. After a draw and two objections at the fielding of ineligible players, the fourth game had to be abandoned when supporters invaded the pitch and began to fight. Violence between rival supporters became so serious during the following season that police erected warning posters at all Irish League grounds.

It was clear from the outset that these incidents had sinister political overtones. Thus, it was scarcely surprising that as political tensions heightened, crowd trouble at matches between Celtic and their Belfast rivals worsened. So against the background of the Home Rule debate, the 1912–13 season was inevitably affected by further violence. In the first match of the season between Celtic and Linfield, a battle between rival supporters resulted in a half-time abandonment. Later in the season, Celtic visited Windsor Park to be greeted by gunfire from the ranks of the Linfield supporters which continued throughout the game (Kennedy, 1989: 21).

The situation in Ireland remained tense throughout the period of the Great War and in its aftermath. Senior football was abandoned to return in 1919–20, once again to the sound of gunfire. At a cup semi-final replay between Celtic and Glentoran crowd violence again resulted in abandonment. After that decision had been taken, a man began to fire a revolver at a stand full of Glentoran supporters. Four people were treated for serious gunshot wounds and others were injured in the rush towards the exits precipitated by the bout of shooting (Kennedy, 1989: 28).

At this stage in Celtic's history the club's directors seriously considered leaving league football. Shareholders succeeded in making them reconsider this decision. Ironically, however, violence and political tension in Belfast during the summer of 1920 were so serious that a general feeling emerged that, although league football should go ahead in the following season, the presence of the Dublin clubs, Shelbourne and Bohemians, together with Belfast Celtic would serve to exacerbate an already grave situation. As a result, the League Management Committee agreed that these three clubs should withdraw from the Irish League temporarily and Celtic were denied senior football until season 1924–25.

Controversy continued to surround Celtic fixtures throughout the remainder of the club's ill-fated history. Equally striking, however, is the success which the team enjoyed on the field of play. In total, 14 league championship triumphs were recorded, together with eight victories in the Irish Cup and numerous lesser awards. Belfast Celtic's record was surpassed only by that of Linfield, and the intense rivalry between the clubs added potency to a situation already charged by sectarian ingredients. It was almost inevitable, therefore, that the eventual departure of Belfast Celtic from the Northern Irish football scene was precipitated by events which took place at a match between the two clubs at Windsor Park on Boxing Day, 1948.

In the first half of the game Linfield's Bob Bryson suffered a broken ankle in an accidental collision with Celtic's Jimmy Jones. The game ended in a 1–1 draw. The events which took place after the final whistle, as explained by John Kennedy, are what the match is now remembered for.

> As the Celtic players were leaving the pitch on their way to the pavilion, they were mercilessly attacked by a section of the crowd and had to literally run for their lives. During his anxious attempt to escape, the unfortunate Jimmy Jones, who seemed to be a particular target, was pushed over a parapet on to the terracing. Here he was set upon so savagely that it was feared he would never kick a ball again. He suffered multiple bruises, had his leg broken, and had to be carried in an unconscious state to the dressing room. (Kennedy, 1989: 92)

Other Celtic players were also attacked. Afterwards the Linfield board and numerous Linfield supporters expressed their disgust at what had taken place. The damage, however, was done.

Belfast Celtic's directors decided that in order to prevent any further incidents of such gravity the club would withdraw from the Irish League at the close of the current season. On 21 April 1949, permission to withdraw was granted and Crusaders were invited to replace Celtic for the 1949–50 season. In the summer of 1949 the club embarked on a highly successful tour of the United States and Canada, which included a 2–0 victory over the Scottish international side. Never again, however, did Belfast Celtic compete in Irish League football and the Celtic Park site of some of the club's greatest moments is now occupied by a shopping complex. Could Celtic's fate have been avoided? Kennedy is doubtful:

> The sad fact of the matter is that the Belfast of the late Forties was no different from that of the early Twenties or the Eighties. The rivalry between Belfast Celtic and Linfield was simply too intense to be healthy. A match between the two teams always held the potential for serious spectator violence. (Kennedy, 1989: 97)

So what was to be done?:

> The only way to remove the threat was for one of the teams to withdraw from the Irish League. Sadly, from the point of view of their supporters, it was the Celtic Board which took the unpalatable but necessary decision. By doing so, they undoubtedly saved an untold number of people from being seriously injured. (ibid.)

Nevertheless, Celtic's disappearance did not signal an end to sectarian incidents in Northern Irish football. Linfield, a club which in the past had employed Catholic players and members of staff despite an over-whelmingly Protestant support, became increasingly exclusively Protestant. Indeed, the club's intense rivalry with Glentoran is partly geographic, with the two drawing support from different areas of Belfast, and partly doctrinal, given Glentoran's continued willingness to employ Catholics, a policy fully accepted by most of the club's Protestant supporters. As a result, some Catholics turned to Glentoran on the demise of Celtic. What they wanted, however, was a team, like Celtic, which would be universally acknowledged to be their very own.

For a short period, Catholic supporters were attracted to Distillery Football Club as a possible substitute for Celtic. As a consequence, and also due to the sensitive location of the club's Grosvenor Park home ground, trouble began to erupt at Distillery matches. In 1972, the club was obliged to leave Grosvenor Park and assume a nomadic existence, playing at a variety of Belfast venues until a new home was established near Lambeg on the southern outskirts of the city.

By the end of the 1970s, Belfast's Catholic supporters had turned their attention to Cliftonville Football Club, which had been for many years an amateur side totally devoid of any sectarian identification. Indeed, in terms of ownership, administration and employees, Cliftonville has continued to eschew sectarianism. However, because the club's ground, Solitude, is located close to Catholic areas of north Belfast it was adopted by local Catholics and, in due course, came to receive the support of Catholics from other parts of the city. The restricted level of achievement reached by Cliftonville over the years made the club seem like a poor substitute for the mighty Celtic. But in 1979 Cliftonville won the Irish Cup for the first time in 70 years and acquired a substantial, almost entirely Catholic, following in the process.

The size of Cliftonville's support varies markedly in accordance with the team's fortunes. What is guaranteed, however, is that it is always large and vociferous when the club faces the old rivals, Linfield and Glentoran. Security measures taken for these games, however, are generally sufficient to prevent serious crowd trouble. Indeed, as part of its security policy, the Royal Ulster Constabulary demands that Cliftonville must play all 'home' games against Linfield at the latter's Windsor Park ground. In addition, at the beginning of 1990, the R.U.C. also advised the I.F.A. that matches between Cliftonville and Glentoran at Solitude should be played in the afternoon and not under floodlights. There has been trouble at Cliftonville matches, the 1979 Irish Cup final included, but ironically the most serious disturbances to occur during a match involving the club took place when Cliftonville played Glasgow Celtic in a friendly game in 1984. The irony lay in the fact that the supporters of the two teams involved were either the same people or, at worst, would be on good terms with their rivals. The disturbances were the result of the hostile response by supporters of both sides to what seemed an unnecessarily large security presence, particularly given the tense atmosphere in Belfast at the time. A few days earlier a man from the west of the city had been killed by a plastic bullet fired by an R.U.C. officer during a Republican rally attended by Martin Galvin, a leading member of the American republican fund-raising organisation, NORAID. The very presence of a large contingent of police officers at a sporting gathering attended almost exclusively by Catholics was insensitive to say the least. Many supporters decided to vent their rage on the R.U.C. during the game and ensuing trouble culminated in the use of plastic bullets once again.

It must be recognised, of course, that ordinary football hooliganism is also present in Irish League football. Indeed, scenes at games between Linfield and Glentoran, notably the Irish Cup Final of 1983, have been much worse than those usually associated with Cliftonville. But the fact remains that for the security forces, while all forms of hooliganism are unacceptable, only those which occur in an identifiable inter-community context are potentially threatening to civil order. Only in this way can the strange history of Derry City F.C. be properly understood.

Derry (or Londonderry) is a predominantly Catholic city and yet Gaelic sport has never enjoyed the popularity reserved for association football. Derry City Football Club was first admitted to the Irish League in 1929 and from time to time matches between the club and Linfield were marred by violent scenes (Platt, 1986). On the whole, however, the club managed to avoid sectarian labelling and received considerable support from both communities. Derry City won the Irish Cup on three occasions (1949, 1954 and 1964), as well as the Irish League (1965) and numerous minor honours.

Despite occasional crowd incidents, the club's travails did not really begin in earnest until rioting broke out in the city in 1969. The club's ground, the Brandywell, is located close to the nationalist Bogside area. This made it an uninviting place for Protestant supporters of Derry City and also for other Irish League clubs and their followers. Furthermore, large numbers of the latter simply added to an already difficult security problem in the city.

In 1971 matters came to a head when rioting during and after a match culminated in a mob setting fire to the bus which had brought Ballymena United officials and players to the Brandywell. Derry City's directors decided that the club should play the remainder of the season's 'home' fixtures at Coleraine's ground, almost 40 miles away. It became apparent that in the light of continued civil strife and political uncertainty, an early return of Irish League football to the Brandywell was unlikely. Worse still, as a result of debts incurred because of playing these 'home' games away from the city, the decision was taken to suspend operations completely.

Consequently, for many years senior football remained absent from Northern Ireland's second city despite regular discussions about the possibility of Derry City's return to the Irish League. Ultimately the security problem was always raised as the major stumbling-block.

Once it became clear that this problem was unlikely to disappear in the near future, a number of Derry City enthusiasts arrived at the conclusion that an application to join the Dublin-based F.A.I. was the only hope if senior football was to return to the Brandywell. Application for admission to the League of Ireland was accepted and Derry City entered the First Division of the League in 1985. Promotion to the Premier Division was secured in season 1986–87. Derry City have also won the League of Ireland Shield in 1986 and the League Cup in 1988, and in 1988 the club were beaten finalists in the F.A.I. Cup. In 1988–89 Derry City won the Premier Division championship, thereby gaining access to the 1989–90 European Champions' Cup. In short, the most successful and best-supported club playing football in the Irish Republic during the second half of the 1980s was from Northern Ireland, where it is barred from participating in organised league and cup football.

The afternoon of 13 September 1989, witnessed the climax of one of the most intriguing sagas in the history of assocation football. Derry City Football Club played Portuguese League Champions Benfica in a first round tie of the 1989–90 European Champions' Cup and, in so doing, became the first team to represent two different national leagues in this prestigious tournament. Derry City faced Benfica as reigning champions of the League of Ireland, administered from Dublin and contested, with the exception of Derry, by clubs based in Dublin and elsewhere in the Irish Republic. In the 1965–66 European Cup, however, Derry had played F.K. Lyn of Oslo in a preliminary round and Belgian champions, Anderlecht, in the first round proper, as the representatives of the Irish League. Furthermore, in season 1990–91, for the first time in its history the League of Ireland's League Cup Final was played outside of the political boundaries of the Irish Republic at Derry City's ground. For some, the current buoyant state of football in the city of Derry might be regarded as one of the happier products of the collision of sport and politics in Ireland. In a perverse way, the Troubles and their particular impact on the city of Derry may have contributed indirectly to the successful rehabilitation of association football there.

Derry City now has relatively few Protestant followers compared with when the club was at its most successful in the Irish League. Some Protestants object to the fact that League of Ireland games are played on Sundays in defiance of Lord's Day observation. Others are simply frightened to enter nationalist areas of their city and thus regard Derry City's ground as a no-go area. Most, however, have come to regard Derry City as a nationalist club *per se*, with few Protestant players or officials and little desire, or financial need, to attract Protestant followers. In the club's defence it might be argued that it is the political context which has forced it into a nationalist ghetto, in a real and a metaphorical sense. In addition, with the managerial appointment in 1991 of Roy Coyle, a former Linfield manager, Derry City have given a strong signal that the club is not sectarian. Such gestures, however, mean little to Protestants in Derry and elsewhere in the north west of the Province. Most of them express their feelings simply by staying away from the Brandywell. The hooligans among them, however, lie in wait ready to throw missiles at busloads of Derry City supporters as they return from games in the Irish Republic.

Thus, the impact of the Province's political turmoil generally continues to be negative as regards the development of the game domestically. Reflecting on the implications of the crowd disturbances at their 1990 Irish Cup tie with Linfield, officials of Donegal Celtic, who had previously entertained hopes of gaining admission to the Irish League, recognised that this would be impossible in the present political and security context, and stated that they would be investigating the possibility of following the example set by Derry City and seeking entry to the League of Ireland.

This particular fixture had created deep controversy long before the referee's whistle blew to commence proceedings on the field of play. The cup draw itself had dictated that Donegal Celtic, an Intermediate League club based in nationalist west Belfast, would have home advantage against Northern Ireland's major club, Linfield. On the advice of the R.U.C., the I.F.A. decided that the game should be played at Windsor Park where the police believed potential trouble would be more easily contained. Partly in the interests of survival in the competition, but also because of their antipathy towards the connotations of loyalist supremacy which Windsor Park symbolises, Donegal Celtic sought a High Court injunction to have the I.F.A.'s decision reversed. This action failed largely on the basis of the R.U.C.'s insistence that they could only ensure the protection of public order and safety if the game were played at Windsor Park. As it turned out, serious crowd violence took place during the match with the result that 48 policemen and 15 civilians were reported injured, and police officers took the decision to fire plastic bullets in order to quell a disturbance which spilled out of Windsor Park and led to a night of rioting and bus burning in nationalist areas of the city.

One can only speculate as to the possible repercussions had the fixture been permitted to go ahead at Donegal Celtic's own ground in Andersonstown. But what is beyond doubt is that the R.U.C. failed totally to ensure public safety when the game finally went ahead at the venue of their choice. The reaction of the leading nationalist newspaper in

Northern Ireland was predictable enough:

> The type of attitude displayed by some of the police, and witnessed by representatives of this newspaper at Windsor Park on Saturday, specifically in relation to the various plastic bullet incidents, and in their general reaction to the trouble caused by segments of the Linfield following, must give rise to grave disquiet. (*Irish News*, 19 February 1990)

However, according to the *Irish News*, responsibility for the failure to ensure security and order should be shared with the R.U.C. by the I.F.A. and their 'disgracefully cavalier attitude in riding roughshod over the views of the Donegal Celtic management in choosing, without full consultation with the Club, Windsor Park as the venue for a game which was always going to be volatile on and off the pitch' (*Irish News*, 19 February 1990). In the view of journalists, there was 'a smug complacency bordering on triumphalism emanating from Windsor Avenue [site of the I.F.A. headquarters] in the aftermath of last week's High Court ruling in favour of the I.F.A.'. The logical conclusion for nationalists to draw was obvious:

> The Irish Football Association took it upon itself, along with the police, to choose Windsor Park. It cannot now abdicate responsibility for its misjudgement and the subsequent mishandling of the game. (ibid.)

Thus, the incidents which happened at a football match were propelled into the public domain of Northern Irish politics. Indeed, the political tension which events of this kind can cause was recognised by the leading Unionist newspaper in the Province, which on this occasion echoed many of the sentiments exhibited by its rival publication as it expressed disquiet at how the fixture had been handled.

Although Unionist politicians were quick to apportion most of the blame for what had taken place to Donegal Celtic and those who had decided to lend their support to that club for the day, the *News Letter* pointed out that, 'on a day which brought shame to soccer and to hundreds of hangers-on the lesson to be learned for the future is that where serious trouble is anticipated on anything like the scale witnessed on Saturday the problem is not readily solved by the expedient of switching the venue!' (*News Letter*, 19 February 1990). The *News Letter* claimed not only that the I.F.A. had handled the pre-match controversy badly, but also that serious questions needed to be asked about police strategy and tactics. These concerns were expressed by the paper in an attempt to prevent opinion about what had occurred at the Irish Cup tie from being polarised on sectarian grounds. Inevitably, however, among the population at large comments on the events were just as sectarian and just as polarised as had been the two rival groups of supporters on the day of the game.

During the 1990–91 season history almost repeated itself when, once more in the Irish Cup, Donegal Celtic were drawn at home against another senior club, Ards. While Ards do not invoke the loyalist imagery of Linfield, the majority of their supporters are Protestants. Despite the lessons of the previous season and notwithstanding the relatively low political profile of the Ards' supporters, the R.U.C. deemed that it would be too great a security risk to allow the fixture to take place in west Belfast and insisted, with the cooperation of the I.F.A., that the game be switched to Ards' ground in Newtownards, 12 miles south east of Belfast. This proved to be too much for Donegal Celtic's management committee who decided to withdraw from the competition altogether. Celtic's pariah status was confirmed at the end of the season when their application to play senior football in the League of Ireland was rejected. Even though Derry City had created a precedent for Northern Irish clubs playing in the League of Ireland, the prospect of senior clubs from the Republic and their supporters crossing the border and journeying into the heart of Belfast was considered to be too risky by southern officials. Thus, because of the politics of division in Northern Ireland, Donegal Celtic are literally the club that nobody wants.

The supreme irony, of course, is that had Donegal Celtic been admitted to the League of Ireland they, like Derry City, would have been regarded as disloyal for having entered a foreign league, despite the fact that those who would have been most vociferous in their accusations would have been least likely to welcome the involvement of these clubs in the Irish League. The cumulative effect of all of this is to make the integrative potential of football increasingly difficult to realise, especially in Belfast.

One reason why it is highly unlikely that Donegal Celtic or teams of a similar complexion and location will ever be admitted into senior football in Northern Ireland, is the fact that the R.U.C. has one of the U.K.'s most outstanding police football teams playing locally in the Irish League 'B' division. This division is one step below senior status and traditionally any team wishing to join the Irish League must first be admitted to and win promotion from the 'B' division. The security situation rules out the prospect of an R.U.C. team making regular, publicly scheduled visits to nationalist areas of west Belfast. This means that regardless of proven ability, unless the R.U.C. withdraw from the 'B' division, teams like Donegal Celtic will never be allowed to fulfil their potential in Northern Ireland. For their part, police officers in Northern Ireland who wish to pursue extra-curricular interests in sport face many problems. If they elect to play in sides outside of the police force alongside civilians whose political affiliations are unknown to them and where total security cannot be guaranteed, they become vulnerable to isolated acts of terrorism. On the other hand, when they choose to play for exclusively R.U.C. teams they become part of a collective entity which is regarded as a legitimate target by Republican terrorists. Hence, all of the R.U.C.'s sporting engagements are carried out beneath an extensive security blanket. This affects officers in a wide range of sporting activities, but given that football is played extensively on both sides of the sectarian divide (as opposed to sports like hockey and rugby) it is almost inevitable that R.U.C. football teams find themselves in situations of the greatest sensitivity. Tight security must then be the order of the day, especially since it is feared that I.R.A. units have already unsuccessfully targetted grounds where the police were due to play. In addition, in the summer of 1989 a visit by a team representing the Irish League to the United States was placed in jeopardy because of nationalist death threats to two serving members of the police force who were in the touring party. Tight security measures were put into operation in order to allow the tour to go ahead.

Despite association football's universal popularity, the history of the game in Ireland, generally, and in post-Partition Northern Ireland, in particular, is replete with instances of sectarian animosity and resultant violence. Players themselves can negotiate the stifling impact of tribal loyalties, at least while they remain on the field of play, but it is doubtful if many change their political allegiances on the strength of having played against or even alongside members of the opposing community. Many supporters, for their part, such as those who followed Linfield to Dundalk in 1979 and caused mayhem, use the sport as little more than a convenient excuse to re-enact the inter-community battles of old and to re-endorse political and cultural prejudices.

Perhaps sadder than any of this, however, is the fact that those who administer the game in Northern Ireland either deny that there is a problem or offer the defence that the difficulties which do occur are wholly outside their sphere of influence. To be fair to them, it is certainly unreasonable to lay society's ills at football's door without looking for fundamental causes – a policy which Mrs Thatcher's Conservative government was all too ready to adopt, as was revealed in its ill-fated Football Membership Scheme Bill. Nevertheless, football administrators in Northern Ireland should be concerned that their sport has been far more dramatically affected by sectarian strife than any other. Two clubs have withdrawn from the Irish League as a direct result of communal violence. Another was obliged to find a new home. The League programme is contested each year with one club, Linfield, enjoying one more home fixture than its rivals and another, Cliftonville, forfeiting a home fixture. In addition, and most conclusively, international matches at Windsor Park have become disfigured by gross sectarian abuse which prompts critical comments, but absolutely no action from the I.F.A.. Despite the claims of the game's administrators that football and politics are separate issues, Catholics in Northern Ireland feel that by doing nothing, the I.F.A. are making a political statement. The following editorial comment in the Province's leading nationalist newspaper, made in the wake of the Donegal Celtic controversy, is a fair summary of this position:

That spineless organisation [the I.F.A.] has failed abjectly in its responsibility, since the departure of Belfast Celtic in 1949, to reassure all fair-minded people that it is an organisation which is prepared squarely to confront the sectarian elements within its jurisdiction, which patently do not espouse equality of opportunity in the playing of football. When will the Irish Football Association start to dismantle the bigot-laden edifice which surrounds the core of the game in Northern Ireland. It is time for the European and World soccer authorities to carry out a close examination of all clubs, particularly those at senior level, affiliated to the I.F.A.. Not until then will we be able to say that soccer in Northern Ireland is a sport where all can use the best facilities and where all can enjoy the world's biggest spectator sport. In the meantime, we have to reconcile ourselves to the fact that in Northern Ireland terms, soccer will continue to stagnate in the foetid waters of sectarianism. (*Irish News*, 19 February 1990)

By their complacent attitude to comments of this type, despite an active commitment to integration at the level of youth football, the administrators of the game in Northern Ireland give the impression that at senior levels, far from being interested in allowing their sport to help the process of community reconciliation, they may actually have a vested interest in maintaining its capacity to divide.

5

SPORT, LEISURE AND THE STATE IN NORTHERN IRELAND: THE ROLE OF CENTRAL GOVERNMENT

There is an enduring voluntary commitment in Northern Ireland to a wide range of recreational and sporting activities. For many years, the Province has had an extensive network of private clubs and associations devoted to golf, racquet sports, various outdoor activities, water sports and a host of individual and team games. Before the 1970s, public involvement in and control over sport and leisure was relatively minimal. Since the onset of the Troubles, however, central and local government have become increasingly engaged in the provision of leisure and recreation in this region to an extent which far exceeds its involvement anywhere else in the United Kingdom. Northern Ireland generally experiences higher levels of social deprivation than most parts of mainland Britain and during the 1970s and 1980s there was an unquestionable need to develop leisure opportunities alongside a range of other public services. It has been argued by some that the expanded leisure provision of this period should be viewed in terms of a sensitive government response to pressing community need. However, it can also be argued that rather than being an expression of a caring welfare state, because this expansion happened during a period of serious civil unrest, leisure in Northern Ireland has been deliberately manipulated by the authorities as a tool of social control, with the objective of undermining, or at least helping to contain, a tendency towards popular urban conflict, particularly among younger Protestants and Catholics. In this and the following chapter we explore these conflicting viewpoints, first, from the perspective of central government and, second, by examining the role of local authorities in general and in Belfast in particular.

This local debate reflects the more general disagreement between British social historians and sociologists as to whether or not public sport and leisure provision have developed as extensions of a largely benevolent welfare state or as elements of an ongoing, and state coordinated, struggle between dominant and subordinate social formations. Over the last 200 years the historical record clearly shows an increasing involvement by central and local government in the free-time activities of the British public (Malcolmson, 1973; Cunningham, 1980). According to Hargreaves (1986) and Clarke and Critcher (1985), the history of working-class leisure in Britain since the industrial revolution is a record of a struggle between capital and labour and the social groupings which this division of labour generated. Coordinated through the state, an informal alliance of politicians, clerics, industrialists, educationalists and the combined forces of law and order targeted the leisure time of an emergent working class. With the rule of law in one hand and an ideological commitment to rational recreation in the other, an attempt was made to entertain the masses and at the same time to discipline their leisure habits, shaping them to complement the needs of a political economy centred around the availability and predictability of a large labour force. The pattern and substance of public leisure provision which have prevailed for most of the twentieth century are seen as the direct products of this late-nineteenth century struggle through which, by and large, capital has triumphed over labour and the leisure habits of the masses have become subject to market forces and state-coordinated control and censorship.

As Bailey (1989) notes, however, establishing the precise motivations behind the state's incursion into popular culture is a very difficult task and one which must look beyond a simple dichotomy between liberal democracy and class struggle. Furthermore, it is equally difficult to establish the level at which officials within the state have been conscious of their instrumental manipulation of the people's leisure and to identify the extent to which this has been a coordinated political strategy. We can be certain that today's leisure infrastructure and the culture it supports is the product of a nexus of competing and complementary social forces, featuring the state and different class groupings, but also including commercial interests, gender relations, regional pressure groups and, increasingly since the 1950s, the influence of racial and ethnic minorities. Indeed, in the last quarter of the twentieth century, British society has gone through significant economic and social change, leading to a reassessment of Victorian strategies for leisure and recreation. As society has become more fragmented, and community-based social order increasingly fragile, it appears that within the network of competing interests identified above, the state has augmented its stake in the use of certain forms of leisure, sport and physical recreation, not only as part of a crusade against falling ethical and moral standards, but also, and perhaps more significantly, as a means of redirecting the rebellious energy of youth and deflecting the discontent of the population in general (Hall, 1986).

In the context of the latter argument, broad parallels have been drawn between the public provision of leisure facilities in Britain's inner cities in the 1970s and 1980s, and the use of the circus within the urban walls of the Roman Empire. This is a rather simplistic argument based on the view that rather than having collective dissatisfaction ferment into open rebellion, together with keeping the population well fed, Rome's imperial rulers utilised the circus as a source of popular gratification and a means of keeping the feared 'mob' physically off the streets and mentally diverted from thoughts of rebellion and revolt. Within modern Britain it is suggested that, through the government's complicity in the sports entertainment industry and high public investment in popular sport and recreation, this strategy of 'bread and circuses' has been resurrected as an ideological support to the state's increasing involvement in the coordination and control of areas of popular culture which were formerly within the realm of civil society. More sophisticated versions of this argument have been developed by critical theorists and Marxist scholars, who include sport and leisure among a range of social institutions through which the state, on behalf of a dominant social class, seeks to maintain an ideological hold over subordinate social groupings (Hoch, 1972; Brohm, 1978).

The main problem with this thesis, however, is the difficulty involved in uncovering empirical evidence in its defence. Since the Second World War, with the possible exception of a short-lived popular revolt in Paris in 1968, nations throughout Western Europe have had few serious problems of order to contend with. A Marxist may argue that this points to the success of the modern capitalist state in pre-empting popular dissent through forms of ideological and institutional manipulation, including 'bread and circuses'. Reductionist arguments such as this notwithstanding, in the absence of widespread manifestations of class struggle and community conflict, it is very difficult to find hard evidence to 'prove' that leisure is being manipulated by the state in the service of social control. Some observers argue that subtle forms of subcultural resistance have been operating in Great Britain's inner cities since the 1950s (Hall, 1986; Hebdige, 1979) and, in the face of Britain's growing problem of public order, there is mounting circumstantial evidence to support the social control hypothesis. For instance, in the early 1980s there were a number of serious outbreaks of civil disorder in many inner-city areas, most notable among them being riots in Brixton, St Pauls,

Toxteth, Handsworth and Broadwater Farm. Since then the proliferation of sports halls, community centres and artificial grass playing surfaces in these areas has been remarkable to behold. While the official view of such developments is that they are overdue responses to genuine community need, equally it could be concluded that the real reason why resources were suddenly made available for inner-city leisure and recreation was as a form of soft policing: an attempt to get potentially troublesome youngsters off the streets and involved in activities through which their behaviour could be observed and reformed and their otherwise destructive energies diverted towards socially acceptable goals. However, if it exists at all, for most of the United Kingdom the social control function of public leisure provision remains largely disguised. In Northern Ireland, however, the extent to which the state, for reasons of security, seeks to involve itself in popular culture in general and sport and leisure in particular is far more visible.

SPORT AND LEISURE PROVISION AND THE TROUBLES

While street disorders such as those in Brixton and Toxteth presented fleeting challenges to public authority, as we have seen, since the late 1960s Northern Ireland has experienced near-constant civil disobedience and on occasions has arguably been on the brink of civil war. In response, the British Government has spent a great deal of money on direct security measures in Northern Ireland, including the maintenance of a large military and police presence. However, direct forms of state control, which rely on penal law and the use, or threatened use, of armed force, are neither cheap nor, in the long term, particularly effective. The least expensive and most effective forms of social control are those which encourage individual members of a population to exercise self-restraint. This is why the British Government has been willing to invest heavily in Northern Ireland's socio-economic environment. It is thought that a robust economic infrastructure could provide the basis for relative prosperity and community stability. Through giving people jobs, reasonable incomes, adequate housing and providing for lifestyles which match this relative prosperity, it is hoped that more of the population may recognise that they have a vested interest in the maintenance of order. In other words, the aims are to remove the socio-economic conditions which, in part, sustain and exaggerate Northern Ireland's political crisis, in order to secure the high ground of hegemony, and to sit back and hope that the Troubles will fade away.

Unfortunately, it has proved to be exceptionally difficult to solve Northern Ireland's economic problems. It is hard to attract long-term foreign investment and the Province has only a small indigenous manufacturing sector. Consequently, unemployment in the region is higher than anywhere else in the United Kingdom. In the absence of basic economic regeneration, there seems to be a belief that by focusing on the lifestyle element of the equation outlined above, some of the problems associated with the Troubles can be weakened. By giving people non-destructive things to do with their spare time and by brightening up their neighbourhoods, it is hoped that they will be diverted from active participation in political violence. It is in this context that the unparalleled expansion of public involvement in sports and leisure provision and administration in the 1970s and 1980s, particularly in the Province's urban areas, must be understood. We begin by looking at the role of central government's main arm of sport and leisure provision in the region, the Department of Education for Northern Ireland.

The Department of Education for Northern Ireland: The Ministry of Sport, Leisure and Culture

While in the rest of the United Kingdom the Government is implicated in the administration of sport, it does not exercise direct control. Rather, through a number of Departments, notably the Department of Environment and the Department of Education and Science, the Government is able to exert influence on quasi non-governmental organisations (quangos) and voluntary bodies and trusts such as the Sports Council and the Central Council for Physical Recreation (C.C.P.R.). It can also wield a degree of authority over the sport and recreation policies of local councils. In Britain there is, of course, a Minister for Sport, but no Ministry of Sport. For instance, in 1990 the Minister for Sport was Robert Atkins M.P., Parliamentary Under Secretary at the Department of Education and Science (with responsibility for sport), indicating that sport was only one portfolio within his junior ministerial brief. The first Minister for Sport was Lord Hailsham, who summed up the ethos of his appointment in 1962 when he spoke of, 'a need, not for a Ministry, but for a focal point under a Minister, for a correct body of doctrine perhaps even a philosophy of Government encouragement' (C.C.P.R., 1991).

The situation in Northern Ireland is somewhat different. In 1972 the devolved powers of the Northern Ireland Assembly at Stormont to administer areas such as economic development, the police, education, health and social services were removed by the Conservative Government of Edward Heath to be replaced by direct rule from Westminster. Direct rule was to be executed through the Northern Ireland Office and a range of statutory bodies and boards staffed by civil servants. Within this arrangement, the leading public responsibility for all things pertinent to physical education, sport and recreation fell within the remit of the Department of Education for Northern Ireland (D.E.N.I.). During the same year, a Local Government Act reorganised the Province's district councils, stripping them of many of their traditional responsibilities, including an input into educational matters. However, in 1973 the Recreation and Youth Service (Northern Ireland) Government Order devolved to the otherwise denuded district councils, statutory responsibility for the provision of 'adequate facilities for recreational, social, physical and cultural activities'. Capital grants to enable district councils to meet such statutory responsibilites were made available from central government, subject to the approval of D.E.N.I.. The same Order also established the Sports Council for Northern Ireland and the Province's Youth Service, placing them both under the control of D.E.N.I.. Later, the Arts Council of Northern Ireland was established and likewise left under the control of D.E.N.I.. Additionally, in 1975, a Government Order authorised district councils in Northern Ireland to acquire land for the purposes of constructing recreational facilities and further empowered D.E.N.I. to make grants to voluntary organisations providing sporting and recreational facilities. Effectively, in all but name, D.E.N.I., through its overall control of a multifarious network of statutory, quasi-governmental and voluntary bodies and its influence in terms of grant aid to local authorities, became Northern Ireland's Ministry of Sport, Leisure and Culture.

School sport in Northern Ireland

A vast network of primary and secondary schools teaching compulsory physical education and games is the most logical apparatus through which central government, through D.E.N.I., should be able to influence the Province's sporting profile. It has long been argued that physical education and sport make an important contribution to character development, socialisation and the transmission of culture. However, a distinctively British approach to this aspect of the curriculum has not been able to monopolise the terrain in Northern Ireland. Here, an anglophile and largely Protestant muscular Christianity has existed alongside a Celtic and recognisably Jesuit appoach to the teaching and playing of sports and games. Ironically, both traditions attribute a remarkably similar ethical content to sport and games. Certainly, the sermonising of Thomas Arnold on the moral and spiritual virtues of physical education are echoed through the expressed sentiments of Irish Catholic church leaders, such as Archbishop Croke in his support for Gaelic games. It is through the contrasting ideological and political meanings assigned to the different contents of an English as opposed to an Irish school sports curriculum, that community divisions in Northern Ireland are compounded. That this continues to happen is largely the result of the Province's divided primary and secondary education system.

The structure of secondary education in Northern Ireland is complex. However, for our purposes it is sufficient to note that through a combination of factors involving methods of funding, degrees of state control, direct and indirect church involvement and territoriality, the overwhelming majority of Northern Ireland's schools can be accurately categorised as either Catholic or Protestant. Schools in the Province do not formally set out to recruit from one section of the community. However, with the tacit approval of both Catholic and Protestant church leaders, there is a long-standing tradition of sectarian self-selection which ensures that the school system remains divided. Thus, the main distinguishing feature of these schools is their relative exclusivity. Obviously, the fact that Protestants are taught alongside Protestants and Catholics alongside Catholics, in separate institutions, is bound to have a limiting effect on the interpersonal horizons of impressionable young people and a negative impact on cross-community relations. In recognition of this, D.E.N.I. has encouraged the development of schools which are formally established with the purpose of drawing pupils from both religious traditions, but to date the movement for integrated education has been of relatively minor significance. In 1992 there were only two integrated secondary schools and just eight integrated primary schools in the whole Province.

Perhaps of more significance are clauses in the 1989 Education Reform Order (Northern Ireland). The central purpose of this order was to launch the national school curriculum as it applied to Northern Ireland. What set it apart from its English equivalent was the establishment of Education for Mutual Understanding (E.M.U.) and Cultural Heritage as cross-curricular educational themes. In the absence of the institutional ability or political will to impose a uniform education system on the Province, these themes are aimed at reducing the impact of segregated education on community relations. Sport and related forms of recreation have emerged as vehicles through which schools hope to meet some of the objectives of E.M.U.. Organising combined sports days, sharing sports tours and joining together to visit leisure facilities and/or areas of geographical and historical interest are some of the means through which groups of Protestant and Catholic schoolchildren have been brought together. However, the effectiveness of ephemeral initiatives such as these is yet to be established. Meanwhile, within mainstream secondary education there remain certain important differences of emphasis in the taught curriculum, particularly in areas such as religious education, languages, history and physical education.

It is the differential promotion of sports and games detailed in the first three chapters which helps to reinforce the emergence of separate and sectarian identities for the Province's schoolchildren. In the first place, participating in school-based sport can become for many children an important early indicator that they are different from youngsters from other schools in other communities. Second, we have already noted that sports can provide the foci for subcultures which help to perpetuate those processes of differential socialisation which underpin community division in Northern Ireland. School is the place where most of us establish those sporting preferences which stay with us as players, administrators and supporters for the rest of our lives and provide us with a long-standing network of friends and acquaintances. Witness the large numbers of old boy's leagues and sports clubs which have their origins rooted in schools. Finally, often the structure of inter-school competition can help to exacerbate sectarian tensions between young Protestants and Catholics. This is particularly true of soccer, which is included in the games curriculum of many schools affiliated to both traditions. Potentially healthy inter-school rivalries can be easily spoiled when events beyond the control of the school authorities and league officials turn 'us versus them' league and cup encounters into 'us Catholics versus them Protestants' and vice versa. This tendency is certainly not discouraged by the example sometimes set by adults at senior level.

As part of a study of segregated schools in Northern Ireland, Dominic Murray surveyed games playing and his findings confirm that the sports curriculum tends to be divided according to different cultural associations which 'have traditionally been along lines which might broadly be defined as "British" and "Irish/Gaelic"'. However, he also points out that there are certain sports, such as soccer, basketball and netball, which 'cut across the denominational split' (Murray, 1985: 44–5). Nevertheless, as we have seen in the case of soccer, simply playing a game which is played by people in the other community counts little towards assimilation if it is only done so against them and in the company of those from 'your own side'.

One final illustration underlines the cultural and political complexities which accompany school sport in Northern Ireland. The Irish Christian Brothers are a Catholic teaching order with schools established throughout the world. However, their main strongholds are in the Republic of Ireland, England and Northern Ireland. In Christian Brothers' schools in Northern Ireland Gaelic games provide the lynchpin for the physical education curriculum and are vigorously promoted to the virtual exclusion of the other major outdoor team ball games, namely rugby union, hockey and association football. Most other Catholic secondary schools in the Province adopt a similar practice. Although some will play soccer as a secondary sport to Gaelic, none encourage the playing of rugby union. However, in the Republic of Ireland rugby union is the favoured game in certain Christian Brothers' schools as it is in many schools run by other teaching orders, such as the Jesuits. Indeed, the elite Catholic schools and colleges are important contributors to the grass roots of rugby union south of the border. Compounding this irony, Christian Brothers' schools in England are also famous for their dedication to rugby union. How can this be explained? In the Irish Republic and England, schools operate under circumstances in which national sovereignty and cultural identity are less significant issues than they are in Northern Ireland. In schools which have a largely middle-class intake, the social content of the games curriculum is unambiguously directed towards the encouragement of attitudes, values and symbols of status appropriate for adult life in a middle-class environment. In parts of the Republic of Ireland and throughout England this means that rugby union will be the favoured team game. However, in Northern Ireland, so long as concerns over religion and ethnicity outweigh those connected with social class, Gaelic games will continue to dominate the physical education curriculum in most of the Province's Catholic schools and especially in Catholic grammar schools, wherein this section of the community's future leaders are most likely to be educated. The segregated school system is often unjustly accused of being the source of many of Northern Ireland's social and political problems. However, in the case of the role it plays in teaching and promoting divisions in sport, the school system does seem to have a lot to answer for.

The Sports Council for Northern Ireland

Government interest in sport in the Province is also articulated through the work of the Sports Council for Northern Ireland (S.C.N.I.). It was established in 1973 at the height of the Troubles with the general objective of furthering sport and recreation in the Province. Formerly, this role had been shared rather loosely between the Youth and Sports Committee for Northern Ireland and the C.C.P.R.. After 1973, the S.C.N.I. became the central coordinating agency for sports development in the region. Through three powerful committees, the General Purposes and Finance Committee, the Facilities/Planning Comittee and the Sports Development Committee, and subject to the approval of D.E.N.I., the Sports Council has been able to exercise considerable influence over the Province's governing bodies of sport and the leisure and recreation services of Northern Ireland's 26 district councils.

As an independent body the S.C.N.I. claims to be aloof from the political context of the Troubles. Indeed, after reviewing the 15 annual reports which the organisation published between 1975 and 1990, the reader is left with the impression that the social and political environment within which the S.C.N.I. has been operating during this period has been no different from that of the English, Scottish or Welsh Sports Councils. This is surprising given the levels and frequency of politically motivated community conflict which has been characteristic of this period, and the range of ways in which, directly and indirectly, sport in Northern Ireland has been involved. However, behind campaigns such as Sport For All and the promotion of excellence, the S.C.N.I. makes a significant contribution to the State's endeavours to monitor and control the popular sporting culture of the region.

The institutional ethos which supports the various policies of the S.C.N.I. is characteristically British. The 1982–83 annual report states a common set of objectives for the four regional Sports Councils 'to ensure that the British attitudes and approach to sport are properly represented at the relevant levels of international debate' (S.C.N.I. Annual Report, 1985–86: 6). There are several elements to this ethos. To begin with the S.C.N.I. makes vigorous and regular claims to be apolitical, arguing, as a point of principle, that sport and politics should not be allowed to mix. The most eloquent defender of this position has been George Glasgow, who retired as Director of the Sports Council in 1990 after almost 20 years in office during the height of the Troubles. Mr Glasgow's position has always been that sport in its own right is a force for social good and that the role of the S.C.N.I. is to facilitate and animate sport in society in response to genuine community interests and needs, rather than as a political expedient. He views the examples of political intrigue in sport outlined in the preceding chapters as relatively minor aberrations in the Province's sporting history, and lays the blame for such political intervention and exploitation squarely at the feet of individuals and groups operating beyond sporting boundaries.

Glasgow's successor, Dusty Miller, shares this view. He also maintains that any overlap between sport and politics in the region is restricted to conflict within working-class circles:

> Professional people and the middle class at the end of the day give no thought to this. The Troubles are at the working class, where people are manipulated by interest groups. When your everyday life has been led trying to keep your sanity and body and soul together, it's easy to see how it could be manipulated. (*Sports Illustrated*, 25 November 1991: 16–17)

However, it can be argued that in promoting a particularly middle-class and apolitical view of sport in a society within which all significant aspects of social behaviour in one way or another are bound up with the politics of division, the S.C.N.I. is covertly advancing the political objective of the British government to promote an image of normality, thereby helping to counter nationalist attempts to depict the region as being on the brink of civil war. It remains to be seen whether or not community relations policies developed by S.C.N.I. in 1991–92 represent a significant change in the organisation's view of the social and political context within which it operates.

Certainly, the S.C.N.I. is always willing to help in the promotion of major sporting events, particularly those which attract British and international competitors and media coverage, such as the Ulster Games. John Hargreaves provides us with the following illustration, which is set against the background of the republican hunger strikes and the death of Bobby Sands in 1981:

> The government, recognising the ideological importance of sporting events in this context, put pressure on the Amateur Athletics Association (A.A.A.) not to cancel its championships, which were due to take place in the province the following month. It was decided to launch a counter-propaganda campaign around them to convey the message that Northern Ireland was stabilized. The Minister for Sport attended the meeting personally, together with the Chairman of the Northern Ireland Sports Council and the province's best known athlete, Mary Peters, who also happened to be a member of the Sports Council. The view expressed by these spokesmen, that these championships had brought the community together and that sport was a peace maker, was given great prominence in the media coverage of the event. (Hargreaves, 1986: 201–2)

Furthermore, the S.C.N.I. is dedicated to the stimulation and promotion of sporting excellence at the highest level. That Northern Ireland can continue to produce world famous sporting personalities like Mary Peters and Barry McGuigan to the general acclaim of the population, is presented as a cause for national rejoicing:

> This small country which basks in the glory of so many sports champions and currently reflects on the results of performances in the World Cup and Commonwealth Games can be rightly proud of the achievements of its sportsmen and women. (S.C.N.I. Annual Report, 1985–86: 5)

As in so many other countries, successes on the world stage in athletics, association football, rugby, snooker, motor sports, boxing and so forth are presented as testimony to national fortitude and a reinforcement of the current national boundaries – this despite the fact that it is a dispute over national identity which is at the root of the Troubles. It was the political crisis in South Africa which generated the belief that normal sport is not possible in an abnormal society. While the South African government favoured keeping sport out of the conflict, anti-apartheid groups claimed that allowing sport to go ahead without disruption would create the misleading impression that all was well both on and off the field of play. Similarly, it can be reasonably argued that in promoting a normal image for sport in Northern Ireland the Sports Council is supporting the British Government's desire to present the situation in the Province as 'business as usual', even though the political crisis remains unresolved.

Overlapping with this public relations function and in keeping with the welfarist rationale of the parent organisation, the S.C.N.I. makes expansive claims for the capacity of sport (and by implication itself) to improve the Province's social infrastructure. This it does by encouraging young people to engage in legitimate and disciplined cathartic, physical activities which not only keep them off the streets and drain them of excess energy, but also expose them to a vast array of positive social values. The cumulative effect of participation in sport renders young people more self-controlled and less likely to be drawn into acts of anti-social behaviour, such as vandalism, hooliganism and, worse still, acts of civil disobedience, including association with terrorist groups.

As we have seen in Chapter 2, this is the rationale which persuades the S.C.N.I. to help with the financing of the G.A.A. in Northern Ireland. Given the G.A.A.'s nationalist overtones, the Government is suspicious of its activities and those of its members. On balance, however, encouraging young men to participate in Gaelic sport can still be viewed as a contribution to law and order if it keeps them away from other more socially destructive affiliations. Nevertheless, evidence contained within the organisation's annual reports from 1985 to 1990 suggests that the S.C.N.I. is more comfortable providing financial aid to sports which are rooted in British rather than Irish traditions. Because the G.A.A. in Northern Ireland denies membership to security forces personnel, the S.C.N.I. is constitutionally bound not to provide the organisation with maximum grants and this is used as a justification for the relatively low rates of funding.

A strong tendency towards the British way of doing things is built into the institutional structure of the S.C.N.I.. All four regional Sports Councils are governed by a ruling Council of government-appointed volunteers. John Hargreaves (1986) has argued that the Council membership of the parent organisation links it with the upper reaches of the British Establishment. The same equation operates in terms of the relationship between S.C.N.I. Council members and Northern Ireland's Establishment. The latter is comprised of a commercial and professional elite which is predominantly male and Protestant, and this is reflected in the make-up of the Sports Council's ruling body which is controlled by D.E.N.I. and which is largely made up of businessmen, civil servants, educationalists and a range of other professionals. There have been, and there continue to be, Catholic Council members, but their numbers have never been proportionate to the size of the Catholic community in Northern Ireland. However, it may be an over-simplification to conclude that this in itself provides proof of an anti-Catholic tendency within the S.C.N.I.. For a long time, membership of Government bodies and 'quangos' such as the S.C.N.I. has been condemned by Republican terrorist organisations. In the early 1970s direct threats were made to the lives of anybody who served in such organisations and Catholic members were considered to be particularly vulnerable. Not surprisingly, this affected the numbers of Catholics who put themselves forward for public office and encouraged those who were already members either to withdraw or to keep a low profile. Inevitably, this had an effect on the complexion of the S.C.N.I.'s steering body.

The organisation's complement of around 20 full-time staff is likewise overwhelmingly male and largely Protestant, particularly in the senior ranks. Approximately one-third of the administrative staff employed by the S.C.N.I. since its establishment has been Catholic, an accurate reflection of the size of Northern Ireland's Catholic population. However, policy is shaped at the level of Director, Deputy Director and the two Assistant Directors: posts which have always been held by Protestants. None of this is to suggest that Sports Council officials, be they volunteers or full-time professionals, consciously use their offices in ways which promote sectarian interests. However, institutional structures are often more powerful than individual agencies. Given the dominant ethos of the S.C.N.I., the extent, through D.E.N.I., of the controlling hand of Westminster and the complexion of the organisation's full-time and voluntary workers, it is hard to deny the claims of nationalists that it is one of a number of institutions which assists in the struggle to establish the hegemony of the British state in Northern Ireland.

Community relations

In the late 1980s, D.E.N.I. began to exert its influence on community-based sport and recreation outside of the formal institutional channels dealt with above. Traditionally, the British Government has given priority to three broad areas in its attempt to stabilize the situation in Northern Ireland: security, the economy, and constitutional political processes. Towards the end of the 1980s a fourth area of strategic significance emerged in the form of an increased emphasis on community relations. Throughout the course of the Troubles there have been many local and privately sponsored initiatives aimed at promoting reconciliation between the two communities. However, until the late 1980s such attempts at grass-roots social engineering had not been formally supported by central government. At this time and under the stewardship of Dr Brian Mawhinney, the Northern Ireland Minister for Education, the rise of community relations was singled out as an important strategy for intervention into the culture of dissent which was believed to sustain the Province's political crisis. Mawhinney argued and eventually convinced the British Government that it was pointless to pursue political initiatives in a cultural vacuum. Cross-party talks, the Anglo-Irish Agreement and other attempts to develop dialogue among the various political components of the conflict were doomed to failure so long as large numbers of ordinary Catholics and Protestants in Northern Ireland continued to feel that they had little in common, and much reason to hate one another.

In the context of Northern Ireland 'community relations' may be appealing as an abstract idea, but it is difficult to put the idea into practice. Once more, a large measure of the responsibility for breathing life into this strategy was given to D.E.N.I.. Rather than concentrate responsibility for community relations within a single branch of its operations, D.E.N.I. elected to spread this initiative across a range of its existing agencies and at the same time to establish some new structures specifically designed to boost the profile of community relations. We have already noted that Education for Mutual Understanding and Cultural Heritage were established as cross-curricular themes within Northern Ireland's version of the new national curriculum. In addition, a special community relations division was set up within D.E.N.I. to promote E.M.U.-type activities within and between schools and to animate cross-community contact schemes involving young people outside of regular school hours. Alongside D.E.N.I.'s activities, a special Community Relations Unit (C.R.U.) was set up within the Northern Ireland Office at Stormont, largely to oversee community relations initiatives which are directed towards the adult population. To date, C.R.U.'s activities include the establishment of a quasi-autonomous Community Relations Council (C.R.C.) and the funding of a community relations programme within the 26 district councils.

However, the establishment of a structure for the implementation of a policy on community relations is not, on its own, sufficient guarantee that the objectives of this policy will be met. Almost by definition, community relations work means involving people in situations which require a certain level of interpersonal interaction between those elements of a given community which are experiencing tension and conflict. In the context of Northern Ireland this amounts to discovering ways of bringing together people from the different religious traditions in non-threatening environments wherein they can engage in collective activities in the hope that cooperation will lead to shared understanding, mutual respect and, eventually, community reconciliation.

In recognition of the importance of cultural institutions in forming separate political identities and preventing the development of a harmonious relationship between state and civil society, the Cultural Traditions Group was set up in 1988 by the C.R.C.. The Group's intention has been 'to explore ways of promoting a better understanding of, and a more constructive debate about, our different cultural traditions in Northern Ireland' (Crozier, 1990: vi). In keeping with a long-standing academic tradition which views sport as ephemeral and trivial, sport was not on the agenda of the Group's inaugural conference held in 1989. However, a year later it had become apparent that sport could not be excluded from any discussions concerned with Northern Ireland's cultural divisions. As one of the Group commented:

> The group felt it important, firstly, to endorse the inclusion of a discussion on sport in a conference on Cultural Traditions. Many of the participants recognised sport as an important medium through which culture is expressed and all were in agreement that sport was an agent for communication even though it could, at times, be divisive. (ibid.: 107)

In response, at the Group's second annual conference a seminar was convened, the main focus of which was 'the potential for both producing and reducing division through sport' (ibid.). At this seminar it was recognised that there are many examples of sport being used in a positive way to encourage cross-community relations. However, the group also recognised the divisive nature of sport. Indeed, sport was described as 'an important part of Northern Ireland's problems' (ibid.: 109). While acknowledging the valuable role played by sport in the maintenance of distinctive identities, the seminar expressed fears that the tribalism inherent in such activities as Gaelic sport and rugby union contribute to sectarian animosity. Furthermore, it was suggested that cross-community tensions are exaggerated by association football, which although intrinsically less tribal, has proved to be fertile terrain for the cultivation of sectarian rivalry.

It was recognised that 'sport cannot opt out of the divided society within which it operates' (ibid.: 108). Nevertheless, administrators of sport in the Province were criticised for their lack of sensitivity to or ignorance of the divisive nature of sport:

> They must start looking at the impact of their policies; not just is it good sport, are more people participating; but what impact is it having in a divided society? Is it sectional in its effect? (ibid.: 106)

Finally, the point was made that in Northern Ireland, as in most societies, socio-economic status places constraints on the access of individuals to the whole range of sporting and recreational opportunities. However, access and choice is further limited by the vertical division of

Northern Irish society and by its unyielding sectarian geography. The seminar concluded by making the following series of recommendations:

1. A curriculum for comparative sport could be developed which would maximise the advantages to be derived from diversity in sport by providing the opportunity to sample and become familiar with the full range of sports and the skills involved.

2. Those organisations which share responsibility for provision of sport and leisure facilities must look at ways of 'unlocking' the substantial facilities which already exist to provide access to those who need them most.

3. The governing bodies of sport must begin to look at those aspects of their sports which are divisive and create barriers to cross-community appreciation and participation. They must also seek to maximise the cohesive potential of sport within a divided society.

4. Public agencies charged with responsibility for sport and its development must begin to look at the impact of their policies and deal with any sectional effects they may be having. (ibid.: 116)

While the aspirations inherent in these proposals are laudable, they are by no means all practicable. We agree wholeheartedly that those who administer sport in the Province could do more to help lessen community tension and enhance efforts designed to promote reconciliation. By refusing to acknowledge that sport is intimately bound up with the political crisis, for example, such administrators give tacit support to those who actively seek to use sport for the expression of sectarian values. However, sport is not and can never be a panacea for social cleavages and some of the recommendations are unrealistic. The notion of a curriculum in comparative sport, for instance, is a utopian fantasy in the context of Northern Ireland's existing education system which, with the exception of a handful of integrated schools, operates along strict lines of sectarian division. Furthermore, the idealism of recommendations such as this contradicts the fundamental principle recognised by the Cultural Traditions Group itself, that sport cannot opt out of the divided society within which it operates. It is not sport *per se* which espouses sectarian values. Rather it is the people who play and watch sport who introduce political values into a potentially neutral enterprise. To expect people to affiliate to sport in any way which differs from the manner in which they affiliate to all other areas of social life in the Province is asking a lot. This applies equally to sports administrators, physical educationalists and leisure managers who, in effect, are being asked by the Cultural Traditions Group to 'opt out' of their own divided society to provide the forum within which their fellow citizens can be freed from the constraints imposed by sectarian division.

Nevertheless, because by their very nature many forms of sport and related forms of recreation are social activities which are especially appealing to young people, it is not surprising that they have been incorporated into what is rapidly emerging as a community relations industry in Northern Ireland. This was reinforced in 1991 by comments made by the Secretary of State for Northern Ireland, Peter Brooke, in a speech on the importance of community relations:

> We must try to build on the willingness shown by local politicians from both traditions to work together to improve community relations; we must also continue with the important work of implementing the programme of cross-community contact schemes. Other areas where there is clearly scope for further action and where a number of exciting initiatives have taken place recently include the churches, sport and popular culture. (*Northern Ireland Information Service*, 1991)

Clearly, given what has already been said about the divisive impact which sport, in its native cultural setting, can have in Northern Ireland, the contexts of sport-based community relations projects have to be carefully managed and their outcomes evaluated in some detail. Many such projects are currently being supported by D.E.N.I. and other government agencies. It is worth mentioning two for illustration.

The first, which is called Belfast United, is a cross-community sports programme involving soccer and basketball. Essentially, youngsters are recruited from Catholic and Protestant areas of Belfast to be trained and coached as members of integrated teams. The fact that both sports involved are already played, albeit usually separately, by both sections of the community provides an important common denominator which is initially measured in terms of interest and skill in the games themselves, but which also serves as an interactive medium for the underpinning community relations work. The highlight of the Belfast United project involves residential playing/coaching experiences in the United States. The youngsters are required to live with American families in mixed pairs (Catholic and Protestant). Project evaluations have shown that it is during these extended periods away from home, in the intimate company of peers from a different religious background, that the best community relations work can be done (Sugden, 1991).

The second example is an experiment which is attempting to introduce rugby union to Belfast's Catholic community. In this case a number of Catholic secondary schools and non-rugby playing Protestant secondary schools have been encouraged to send teams to Malone Rugby Club to participate in a series of tournaments using a simplified form of the game. From these tournaments three integrated rugby teams have been selected (under-18s, under-16s and under-14s) and are currently playing regular junior rugby on Saturday mornings in Belfast, as well as going on tour together. This project is especially significant because it requires persuading Catholic youngsters to take up a sport which in Northern Ireland, as we have seen, is clearly associated with a British cultural tradition.

The range and number of community relations programmes which use sport in the ways outlined above will continue to expand so long as government and other agencies are willing to provide the finance. It would be a mistake to make grand claims as to the impact such programmes are having on community relations in the Province. Nevertheless, it is quite clear that these practical, grass-roots experiments in social engineering can have some impact on the relatively small numbers of individuals who experience them. The view taken by many of those who are involved in the development and supervision of such initiatives is that after a quarter of a century of serious sectarian violence and in the absence of any impending political panacea, this very gradual grass-roots work is the only way forward. At least it is better than doing nothing.

There is, however, another way of assessing the function of sport-based community relations work. The people involved in projects such as those outlined above make vigorous claims to have objectives which are fundamentally apolitical. Nevertheless, if government thinking remains the same and the move away from municipally financed mass leisure continues apace, it is increasingly likely that support for these smaller scale activities will be the favoured means through which the state seeks to use sport in the service of community stability. In this sense and regardless of the motivations of those who organise and instigate projects such as Belfast United and the Malone experiment, if the results of their interventions are a reduction in community conflict, then in nationalist circles sport-based community relations will be interpreted as another form of soft policing. Moreover, if such interventions actually do help to encourage a degree of assimilation between Catholics and Protestants, and in doing so help to provide the cultural foundation upon which a negotiated political accommodation can be reached, both hardline unionists and their nationalist counterparts have cause to view community relations programmes with suspicion.

Central government involvement in sport and recreation in Northern Ireland is more direct and more centralised than it is in other regions of the United Kingdom. This is largely because of the overseeing role played by D.E.N.I.. Nevertheless, this is a relative statement. While central government involvement in sport and recreation in Northern Ireland is more direct than it is in Scotland, Wales and England, there remain many ambiguities in the various sport-related functions of the state and its representatives in the Province. We have already noted the contrasting postures of the security forces and D.E.N.I. in their dealings with the

G.A.A.. The security forces view the latter with only thinly disguised suspicion and disdain and treat members accordingly while, through the machinery of the Sports Council, D.E.N.I. give financial support to the Association's growth and development. Also, there is little unanimity within D.E.N.I. itself. On the one hand, D.E.N.I. continues to support and administer a divided and segregated school system, while on the other, it spearheads a community relations campaign which includes integrated education, Education for Mutual Understanding and a wide range of community relations initiatives, many of which are focused on sport (N.I.C.E.D., 1988). These examples show how delicate the balance between force and consent is in Northern Ireland. Central government is obliged to pursue a wide range of strategies – many of which, at least on the surface, appear to contradict one another – in order to maintain a minimum level of order, while at the same time it attempts to resolve the Province's political crisis.

6

LOCAL GOVERNMENT SPORT AND LEISURE PROVISION: THE BELFAST EXPERIMENT

Although for the sake of clarity of explanation we have chosen to deal with local government involvement in sport and leisure separately from that of central government, in fact the two levels are intertwined. Through its Facilities Planning Sub-Committee, the S.C.N.I. had a considerable impact upon the shaping of the sport and leisure facilities provided by district councils in Northern Ireland in the 1970s and 1980s. Given D.E.N.I.'s relationship with the S.C.N.I. and the Department's direct control over capital spending in this area, it was D.E.N.I. which had the leading role in determining the extent of the state's expansion into public recreation in the Province. Nevertheless, in practice it has been the district councils who have been instrumental in determining the shape of that provision. This is largely because, unlike the situation in the rest of the U.K., where local authorities have a remit for community provision of leisure services without being bound by statute to provide them, the 1973 Recreation and Youth Service (Northern Ireland) Government Order requires by law that the 26 district councils of the Province make adequate public sport and leisure provision.

Prior to 1973, Northern Ireland lagged far behind Britain in terms of the provision of public leisure services. In a Province of more than one and a half million people there was not a single public sports centre or leisure centre. Approximately half of these people lived in the greater Belfast area where, apart from a handful of ageing wash-houses and swimming pools, there were no significant indoor sports facilities. The general public had to rely on access to church halls, boys' clubs or, ironically, British army sports facilities if they wanted to participate in activities such as badminton or basketball. There were several public parks which supplemented the streets as playgrounds for the city's young and old alike. In short, before the Troubles, Belfast had to make do with a sport and leisure infrastructure which had changed little since the Victorian era.

In 1969 the Belfast Urban Area Plan had acknowledged the impoverishment of the city's leisure facilities and made suggestions for extensive future development. In urban areas throughout the United Kingdom similar proposals were brought forward for the consideration of city councils and central government agencies. But, in cities such as Leeds, Liverpool, Manchester and Birmingham, during a period of economic recession and in competition with other public services such as health and housing, leisure-directed proposals were either shelved or radically pruned. In Belfast, however, not only were similar proposals favourably received, they were extended by local politicians and their advisors in the knowledge that the vast bulk of the capital costs would be met not by local ratepayers, but by the Treasury at Westminster who would later be accused of 'throwing money' at what was essentially a political problem.

When the Troubles began in the late 1960s, annual capital grants paid through the Department of Education to district councils in Northern Ireland for sport and leisure provision were in the region of £0.5 million. By 1983 the figure was close to £7.5 million. The most significant rise occurred between 1973 and 1975 when central government capital expenditure on leisure increased more than threefold. This coincided with the imposition of direct rule from Westminster at a time when both terrorism and general public disorder were at their greatest intensity. Most capital investment in public leisure was directed to those areas worst affected by the Troubles and was almost totally financed by central government. In Belfast alone, in excess of £30 million was raised and spent on an ambitious building programme. Between 1977 and 1984, the city opened 14 new wet and dry sport and leisure complexes and thus became the leading municipal provider for sport and leisure, per capita, in the United Kingdom. In the same period, throughout the Province, in relatively small cities and towns such as Derry, Armagh, Newry, Antrim, Craigavon, Coleraine, Enniskillen, Omagh and Strabane, impressive public leisure facilities came under construction.

It would be an over-simplification to suggest that this expansion in leisure services was directly caused by the Troubles. It is more accurate to say that such developments were caused by a combination of special circumstances, many of which were bound up with the Province's political crisis. Most obvious were the aforementioned social and economic conditions which provided the context for the Troubles. Setting aside Ulster's political problems, the region was, and continues to be, one of the most economically depressed in western Europe. Relative geographic isolation rendered the Province particularly vulnerable to the effects of the economic recession which hit the whole of western Europe in the 1970s. Notwithstanding sectarian strife, Northern Ireland has suffered from a range of social problems which are common to other economically deprived regions. Whether idle hands do indeed work for the devil is open to question, but the emergence of a growing army of jobless young men with plenty of free time in the inner cities was a source of national concern. In the face of a moral panic over the condition of the nation's youth, both central and local government, as we have already suggested, came to see sport and recreation as important structures in a complex operation to try to maintain community order throughout Britain. It is hardly surprising that in Northern Ireland, where youth-related social and economic problems common to those in the rest of the United Kingdom were compounded by widespread sectarian conflict and civil disorder, leisure and recreation gained rapid ground on the political agenda.

For more than a hundred years forms of recreation have been used by government agencies as a means of controlling the free time of young people and modelling their characters. Certainly, the use of sport in the fight against juvenile delinquency has been a well-established and unquestioned maxim operationalised within many of the institutions involved in the rehabilitation of young offenders. However, such enterprises are seldom evaluated in any detail and it is difficult to discover whether or not activity programmes do in fact deter juvenile crime and modify anti-social behaviour (Sugden and Yiannakis, 1987). A lack of such evidence did not stop similar strategies being used in Northern Ireland. In the summers of 1968 and 1969 the first serious civil unrest in the cities of Belfast and Londonderry occurred. The job of the local security forces and later the British Army was complicated by the presence of large numbers of children and teenagers on the city streets who readily adapted largely harmless, institutionalised patterns of gang fighting into more serious forms of sectarian conflict and riot. In an unequivocal attempt to limit youth involvement in civil disorder, the Government at Westminster, through D.E.N.I., made available large sums of money for non-political organisations to provide activity programmes during the summer months for young people between the ages of 15 and 19. Local playleaders and sports organisers, who were committed to community sport and recreation, were delighted by this windfall because it gave them the opportunity to involve thousands of youngsters in a wide range of activity programmes. However, while the motives of those who initially operationalised the government's intentions may have been rooted in perceptions of long-standing community need, there is little doubt that the physical fitness and play needs of the Province's teenagers were marginal to Westminster's main concern to get them off the streets.

In the absence of conclusive research, it is impossible to judge precisely how much impact, if any, the summer schemes had on the Troubles. From a purely recreational point of view they were very successful and tens of thousands of young people participated in them during the 1970s. However, very few of them engaged in cross-community contact and none of them was subject to any form of systematic evaluation. All that can be said is that for a few months and for a short period of time during the day, X number of children were not on the streets of Belfast, but whether or not participation in organised sports and games in the daytime deterred significant numbers from taking to the streets later at night is impossible to discover. Viewed from the government's distant vantage point, the summer schemes had achieved their prime objective of getting significant numbers of young people off the streets, but at best they were considered as temporary, out-of-school diversions. Furthermore, the relative autonomy of community-based play schemes rendered them vulnerable to the exploitation of local interest groups, some of whom, it was feared, may have been actively involved in the politics of division. Moreover, the Treasury could not afford to pay for the summer schemes as well as finance the capital building programme which was favoured by local politicians and local sport and leisure administrators who had a vested interest in the establishment of a permanent and centralised network of recreational provision. For these reasons, the *ad hoc* approach which characterised leisure provision in Belfast until the 1970s, was displaced in the 1980s by an expanding professional empire of public leisure services.

There is no evidence to suggest that those full-time professionals who have had the day-to-day responsibility for developing and running Northern Ireland's public sports and leisure services, are politically motivated in any sectarian sense. However, a combination of circumstances which include the motives of central government, the divisive nature of local government and, above all, the Province's sectarian geography, has ensured that leisure services, particularly in Belfast, have a considerable political dimension. As a consequence of the prorogation of Stormont in 1972, the administration of areas such as economic development, the police, education, health and social services was placed under direct rule from Westminster, to be handled through the Northern Ireland Office and a range of statutory boards and bodies staffed by civil servants directly appointed by and responsible to Whitehall. During the same year, a Local Government Act reorganised the Province's district councils, and at the same time took away many of their traditional responsibilities. Under the new political arrangements, the district councils were deprived of the authority to provide and administer services which had been the focus of conflict between Catholic and Protestant communities, such as planning and housing, and were left with a few, seemingly uncontroversial, areas such as parks and technical services. Local councils were denied the responsibility for leisure services and, in the planning stages, provision was initiated and overseen by central government operating through the Department of Education, which worked with the consultation of selected sport and leisure experts rather than elected representatives.

There is no public record of the discussions which surrounded the decision-making process through which Northern Ireland received and implemented its leisure windfall. However, in 1988, during a BBC2 television interview, Dr Brian Mawhinney, the Minister then responsible for the funding of public leisure in Northern Ireland, admitted that, in the past, leisure may have been used as a means of channelling the energies of young people away from direct involvement in political violence. This view is supported by research carried out for BBC Radio Northern Ireland by David Huntley (1988), who conducted a series of interviews with senior civil servants and others involved in the early days of Belfast's leisure development. Huntley clearly establishes that those involved in the planning of Belfast's leisure services understood that the money was made available by central government first and foremost in the hope that the provision of leisure in some way might offset the tendency towards civil disorder. As one official remarked:

> In the 1970s the money was running out of our ears. The Government saw that it was extremely important to provide facilities in Belfast, because if you got them in there at ten in the morning and kept them in there until late afternoon, they weren't dragging up stones to throw at the police at night. (Huntley, 1988: 44)

A report by the Sports Council in England had suggested that, in an ideal situation, when available public finance matched community need, a city the size of Belfast should have an optimum of eight leisure centres. At a time when throughout the rest of the U.K. few towns and cities came even close to optimum provision, Belfast opened 14 new facilities. A prominent member of the Belfast Leisure Services Committee in the 1970s had no doubt as to why the city had received the capital to build almost twice the recommended number of facilities:

> We set up 14 not 8, because the Sports Council in England who drew up the figures hadn't the problems we had, they didn't have the population massacring themselves. In order to stop the rioting it was agreed that 14 would be needed. (ibid.: 45)

If the motivation for, and undeclared policy behind, the Province's extensive public leisure provision was covertly political, then the manner through which policy was translated into practice further politicised the situation. Whereas the summer schemes had been virtually instantaneous projects, the planning, designing and construction of leisure centres was a much longer process with many more opportunities for local political interference. The Shankill Leisure Centre, for instance, was at the planning stage in 1972, but was not opened officially until 1980. Even before the beginning of the 1980s, however, civil disobedience and popular riot had become less significant features of the Troubles. In fact, by the time all of the larger leisure centres had opened their doors the very character of the Troubles had already changed.

When such facilities were chosen as the cornerstone of the Government's leisure strategy, rioting was a major feature of civil unrest in Northern Ireland, particularly in the inner cities. A high priority was placed on the need to get people, particularly young people, off the streets. By the mid-1970s, the fact that this objective had been achieved could have little or nothing to do with developments in public recreation. It is highly unlikely that the promise of leisure in the 1980s did anything to curb youthful participation in civil disorder in the early 1970s, or suggest to the wider community that politicians were responding decisively to the immediate social and political problems which fed into the Troubles. Rather, the introduction of the British Army, the emergence of a range of heavily armed paramilitary organisations, increased community polarisation and the threat posed by shootings and bombings were among a series of factors which altered the nature of the conflict and dissuaded people from taking to the streets in numbers, as had been their habitual practice in previous years. Thus, at a time when large and expensive leisure centres were nearing completion, one of the central reasons for their existence, the 'Saturday night riot', had all but disappeared.

From the outset of the Troubles, as civil unrest gave way to terrorism and counter-terrorism, an increasing demographic polarisation occurred, particularly in the greater Belfast area with Protestants and Catholics withdrawing, or being forced to withdraw, into their own separate enclaves. Given that part of the justification for funding public leisure facilities in the Province included claims for the potential of cross-community reconciliation through recreation, this presented those responsible for the implementation of local leisure services with a particular set of problems. To begin with, the faint hope that leisure provision could help to secure community integration in a city which had been so bitterly divided for over a century, was fast being diminished by the shifts in population. The problem of where to locate leisure facilities aimed at integration became increasingly acute as the distance between the communities grew wider and areas which traditionally had been neutral were either abandoned or became subject to sectarian colonisation by one or other religious faction. One option was to build on an open site in close proximity to both Catholic and Protestant housing areas. At a time of high tension, this strategy demanded that people leave the perceived safety of their separate neighbourhoods, which offered a traditional range of communal social activities, and travel to public facilities, located outside of the immediate locality, which might be shared by 'the other side'. Such a strategy could never work. In working-class areas of Northern Ireland, once it becomes public knowledge that a given facility is frequented by people of another religious tradition, the facility is categorised as 'one of theirs'. There are exceptions, but they have tended to be under-used by both communities. Maysfield was one of the first centres to be opened in Belfast. Its location on the banks of the River Lagan, near to the city centre and within equal walking distance from entrenched Catholic and Protestant neighbourhoods, suggests that it was developed with a view to promoting a degree of cross-community participation. In any other city Maysfield's location would guarantee optimum use. However, a hundred yards can be a long way in Belfast, and guidelines on leisure centres and catchment areas have to be rewritten for a city so deeply divided. While it has a reasonable turnover from office workers and school groups during the day, Maysfield does not attract significant numbers from the nearest working-class neighbourhoods. As the comparable history of Brownlow Leisure Centre illustrates, this problem is not confined to Belfast. Built on a site between two communities in the new town of Craigavon, Brownlow is regarded as a Catholic centre by the Protestants and as a Protestant centre by the Catholics and, because of its false reputation, it is underused by both traditions. These cases illustrate how threats of violence and the loyalty felt for one's community can easily combine to undermine efforts at integration, especially through recreation.

The alternative to the integrative approach, and the course of action most usually adopted, has been to site leisure centres in the heart of working-class communities which were also identifiable by their sectarian character. Several considerations lie behind this strategy. Policy may have been decided at Westminster, but its implementation was enacted through a series of offices and agencies, which towards the planning and building stages became closer and closer to the divisive currents which are indigenous to the Province. As we have seen, D.E.N.I. was the funnel for government capital, but it relied on both the S.C.N.I. and local leisure services committees for detailed advice and direction. The capacity of local officials to influence the shape of the Province's leisure services was significantly augmented in 1983 when the hitherto largely impotent district councils were given the added responsibility for leisure services. Compared with parks, cemeteries and rubbish collection, leisure services became and remained a priority item on council agendas. The prospect of having one's own or one's party's name associated with the construction of an expensive leisure centre for a given community has served as a powerful incentive for local politicians to argue for the siting of such a facility in their own electoral wards. For instance, in Castlereagh, a district adjoining Belfast, the leisure centre is officially known as the Robinson Centre, in honour of the Democratic Unionist councillor and M.P. who represents that staunchly loyalist area and who was instrumental in having the leisure facility located there.

As local politicians lobby for facilities in their own constituencies, inevitably this means bargaining along sectarian lines. Research by Knox (1989) has shown that the issue of leisure provision in the Province has been seen by many local councillors as one of 'us versus them'; Protestant versus Catholic; Unionist versus Nationalist. This is supported by Huntley's (1988) findings. As one senior civil servant involved at the planning stage commented:

> It was all sort of a political game. If the councillor for Shankill said 'we must have a leisure centre' then the councillor for Falls would say 'we must have one at Whiterock or Beechmount'. It was all very political with councillors all fighting for their own areas. (Huntley, 1988: 47)

Operating from much smaller capital budgets, towns such as Armagh, Antrim and Omagh, have not suffered to the same extent as Belfast and Londonderry because Catholics and Protestants have had no choice but to share the leisure facilities available. There is, however, little evidence to suggest that the existence of a communal leisure facility has done anything to promote community relations in these areas. In the larger cities there is a 'tit for tat' pattern of provision whereby the development of a leisure facility in a loyalist community has been balanced by the development of one of a similar scale in a nationalist neighbourhood. In Londonderry provision straddles the River Fayle, with separate facilities serving the mutually exclusive and hostile communities of the city side and the Waterside. In Belfast, as Knox (1989) observes, of the city's fourteen centres, seven are used almost exclusively by Protestants, five are used almost exclusively by Catholics, and only two can be classified as neutral.

In any other U.K. context, campaigning for leisure services on a platform of community need can be applauded as civic duty, but in Belfast local council constituencies are almost exclusively either Catholic/Nationalist or Protestant/Unionist. Thus, the struggle for scarce leisure resources tends to be carried out along the same sectarian lines as the Troubles. Furthermore, the outcome of the resulting 'tit for tat' provision actually increases community polarisation by giving each tradition yet another exclusive structure of association through which to reinforce separate and mutually antagonistic identities. In parts of Belfast and Londonderry as each new leisure centre has appeared, they have been claimed, at least symbolically, for one side or the other. Certain centres in Catholic west Belfast have had two opening ceremonies. The official openings have been carried out by high-ranking officials of the Unionist-dominated City Council and various civic dignitaries, to be followed by alternative ceremonies led by one or other of the various Republican organisations. In 1984, for instance, because the City Council refused to invite the local M.P. and Sinn Fein leader, Gerry Adams, to the opening of Whiterock leisure centre, Sinn Fein arranged an unofficial opening which was presided over by Mr Adams and which featured the unveiling of a plaque in Gaelic and the hoisting of the Tricolour. Incensed by the lack of response to this display of nationalism, a Democratic Unionist councillor, the late George Seawright, decided to take the law into his own hands:

> The councillor, brandishing a legally held pistol, mounted an overnight sortie and removed the Tricolour from the Whiterock centre on 18 October 1984 . . . The number of Tricolours at the centre doubled after the nocturnal raid by Seawright. (Knox, 1989: 162)

In keeping with this process of divided identification, the Union Jack and various Loyalist flags have been hoisted on top of centres in Protestant districts. Ironically, councillor Seawright, who was notoriously outspoken in his criticism of all things Catholic, was later assassinated by Republican paramilitaries as he sat waiting in his car in the carpark of the Shankill Leisure Centre, under the shadow of the Union Jack. Elsewhere in the United Kingdom the opening of a leisure centre would probably not be considered as a political act, but such episodes once more illustrate that in Northern Ireland few things are immune from the Troubles and leisure provision is certainly no exception to this general rule.

A seemingly inexorable drive to expand the boundaries of the Province's public leisure services within the contours of division has exaggerated their political profile. Once a large bureaucratic structure is brought into being it tends to develop a vitality beyond the range of its initial objectives. This rule can be applied to many aspects of leisure services throughout Northern Ireland. The impetus for an expanded public sector in leisure came from central government at the beginning of the Troubles as part of a response to the Province's social and political turmoil. By 1983 the responsibility for provision of leisure was handed back to the Province's 36 district councils which, as we have seen, had a very limited remit after the imposition of direct rule. Leisure provision became one of the main career structures within local government and, in keeping with the bureaucratic rule cited above, has succeeded in expanding its boundaries ever since, becoming one of Northern Ireland's major employing agencies. Certainly, as long as central government was content to foot the bill, local government was equally content to build new facilities and see the public sector leisure empire grow, even if it meant following existing lines of community division.

Knox's research (1989) confirms that local councillors understand the political sentiments behind central government's original reasons for funding an extensive programme of leisure centre provision, but dismiss notions of integration through leisure as unrealistic and financially untenable. Westminster may have provided the bulk of the capital to build the leisure centres, but it is the ratepayers who have to pay for their day-to-day running costs. In this regard, the capital windfall of the 1970s has turned into a considerable burden for Belfast's ratepayers. Even with the existing policy of building facilities in the heart of mutually antagonistic neighbourhoods, it currently costs the city £8.4m, or £28 per head per year, to keep the doors open, the floors clean, the pools heated and so forth. As we have noted, even if a sufficient number of neutral sites could be found, it is highly unlikely that facilities in such areas would be used extensively by either tradition, further increasing the ratepayer's burden and undermining the political tenure of those officials responsible for leisure services. Moreover, local politicians and leisure professionals rightly view as naive the suggestion that a leisure centre in no-man's land would stimulate a lasting truce by encouraging otherwise deeply entrenched combatants to set aside their differences and come together in the name of recreation. In the early 1980s, Belfast's Leisure Services Department initiated a series of leagues and competitions between the various centres in the hope that this would result in an atmosphere of sporting fraternity which could transcend sectarianism. Unfortunately, this experiment in cross-community relations had to be abandoned because of the hostility which accompanied some of the fixtures. A serious disturbance between rival factions after a basketball competition at Avoniel leisure centre in East Belfast could only be suppressed with the assistance of the Royal Ulster Constabulary and the Army. After this incident official efforts to integrate leisure centre users ceased. As Huntley (1988: 81) concludes, 'promoting a sporting solution to what is essentially a political problem, is an unrealistic burden to place on leisure centre provision'.

Thus, in terms of optimum participation and revenue generation, the unofficial apartheid which characterises much of Belfast's leisure provision can be viewed as a pragmatic response to the city's uniquely divided community structure. Within this framework it would be unjust to accuse those who run the service with sectarianism.

Indeed, a report by Roberts (1989) compliments Belfast Leisure Services, pointing out that while they may be something of a burden to the ratepayer, judged in terms of participation rates they are more successful than those of comparable cities in Great Britain. This is hardly surprising since unlike the situation in comparable cities, in Belfast, because of the practice of building within sectarian territories, there is a leisure centre on nearly everybody's doorstep. Despite Roberts' encouraging remarks, however, and while recognising that in Northern Ireland administrators are constrained by the sectarian structures within which they operate, O'Dowd *et al.* (1980) caution that 'to equate the absence of sectarian intentions with the absence of sectarianism is a mistake. Sectarian geography may determine the nature [of public leisure provision] more surely than the intentions of the actors'. Thus, regardless of the neutrality and professionalism of administrators and despite the comparatively high participation rates, one effect of Belfast's purportedly pragmatic leisure provision is to shore up the institutionalised sectarian divisions which keep the Province close to the edge of civil war. As such, any hope that central government may have had that by providing capital for leisure it could in some way improve cross-community relations has turned out to be misguided.

Whether or not Northern Ireland's expansive leisure provision has had any impact on the nature and intensity of the Troubles is a different issue. Serious political strife and violent confrontation are still very much a part of life in the Province and there are few indications that the situation is likely to improve. Defenders of Belfast's saturated provision tend to take the view that matters would be even worse if it was not for the attractions of local leisure centres, taking great heart from the fact that random youthful rioting is not as prominent a feature as it was 20 years ago. As we have pointed out, however, the nature of the Troubles had changed from civil disobedience in the direction of terrorism before the first leisure centres were opened. According to Roberts (1989), youth participation rates in leisure centres are higher in Belfast than in comparable cities, but according to local government officers they are still very low. Roberts' Belfast findings notwithstanding, it is generally accepted, by him and by other researchers, that working-class teenagers who are most at risk from involvement in urban disorder, are not predisposed to involvement in forms of organised recreation of any kind (Roberts, 1983). Furthermore, there is no clear evidence to suggest that those young people who use leisure centres are less likely to become involved in civil disorder and other forms of anti-social behaviour. Mass demonstrations, marches and riots have not disappeared altogether as features of the Troubles, and the presence of leisure centres seems to have done little to prevent a return to the streets by lean and fit young men of both communities as the season or the situation may demand.

There are signs that there has been a change of heart and the cost-effectiveness of public leisure services in Northern Ireland is being increasingly called into question. Roberts (1989) suggests that the relative success of Belfast's leisure services in keeping the population healthy and improving community spirit is worth the £28 per head spent on behalf of the city's ratepayers. This view is not shared by the city's auditors' Value For Money Study, which, in March 1989, was highly critical of the scale of Belfast's public subsidy of sport and leisure facilities. For instance, for the 17 leisure centres and swimming pools operated by Belfast in the financial year 1988–89 every paying customer was subsidised on average to the tune of £3.50. In one centre, Shaftesbury, the subsidy was as high as £6 (*Belfast Telegraph*, 21 March 1990). In response to these figures, Belfast Department of Leisure Services have initiated a cost-cutting programme which has led to the closure of the Stadium Leisure Centre, the closure of Ormeau Swimming Pool and the hiving off of Templemore Baths to a community users' association. Other centres have had their opening hours reduced, and in general staffing levels have been cut and prices raised. Belfast Leisure Services view these measures as an exercise in good housekeeping, but local politicians see it as the inevitable price to be paid for mistakes made in the past. As reported in the *Sunday Life* (7 January 1990), Ulster Unionist City Council leader, Fred Cobain, said that these cutbacks were necessary to prevent a rates increase, warning that in the future more centres may have to close. He said the council was burdened with the increasing costs of maintaining and running the centres, which were originally built because of a 'sectarian policy' by central government:

> Central government provided the money to build them on a sectarian basis – one for a green area and one for an orange, and so on – rather than on the basis of need. But the city council has been left to pick up the bill for the running costs.

There has been widespread criticism from other major political parties over proposed cuts in services and resultant redundancies. Both the Alliance Party and the Social Democratic and Labour Party (S.D.L.P.) have argued that leisure centre provision is essential to the health and well-being of the city and that economies should be made elsewhere. Sinn Fein have used the budget crisis as an opportunity publicly to ridicule the Unionist-dominated City Council for its mismanagement of public funds to the detriment of Catholics. According to Sinn Fein councillor, Mairtin O Muilleoir, among a list of 'glaring mistakes', Belfast Leisure Services have failed to provide a leisure centre in nationalist north Belfast, even when government grant aid of £1 million was available. Also, he argues that the city has failed to respond to the success of the ice-bowl in neighbouring Dundonald because of the Unionist-dominated council's preoccupation with its stand against the Anglo-Irish Agreement:

> The Unionists are intent on steering a course which spells disaster for leisure centre staff and users. Their record is a shameful one and proves their inability to properly manage the annual budget of £8 million-plus or properly plan for the future. If the Unionists had have spent as much time consulting with ordinary people about the leisure service as they have spent on junkets or on banning Irish signs in Andersonstown, then the city's leisure provision would not be in the mess it is in today. (O Muilleoir, 1989)

The position is likely to become more complex in the foreseeable future as the government's plans for the privatisation of leisure services are implemented in the Province. The introduction of Compulsory Competitive Tendering (C.C.T.) raises two additional political dimensions. First, with some justification, Unionist politicians have argued that the piecemeal selling off of any aspect of public services in Northern Ireland presents opportunities for the commandeering of important ground in the Province's political economy by antagonistic political and paramilitary associations. Fears have been voiced in council chambers throughout the Province that a loosening of state control could lead to the exploitation of leisure services by anti-government organisations such as the U.D.A. and the I.R.A.. While in the rest of the U.K., many city councillors fight C.C.T. on the grounds of public welfare and the need for protected community services, it is indicative of the impact of the Troubles on all walks of life that in Northern Ireland official resistance to the privatisation of leisure is conducted as part of a broader fight against terrorism.

Secondly, at a more general level, the government's commitment to privatisation and cost-effectiveness on the one hand, and the use of leisure as a medium for social control on the other, illustrates how the state can operate at cross purposes. Already, the threat of C.C.T. has led to a degree of rationalisaton of public leisure services in the Province. Once privatisation takes place, it can be assumed that market forces will encourage further rationalisation, involving even greater reductions in the range of facilities available and increased prices. As we have argued, however, leisure services in Belfast were never intended to make a profit. On the contrary, they were heavily subsidised by the state in the belief that adequate recreation facilities could in some way act as a counterbalance to subversive political action. Either the state is consciously and uniformly abandoning its enduring commitment to the social control function of leisure or, as is more likely, there is an unconscious ideological contest taking place between its welfarist and its monetarist wings, which, for the time being, the latter is winning. If, as Roberts

(1989) suggests and one branch of government clearly used to believe, leisure has had a calming effect on the Troubles, as centres are forced to close their doors in anticipation of privatisation the state may be forced to spend its savings on increases in direct forms of security and control such as the army and the R.U.C..

Outside of Northern Ireland, it has been argued that the state's strategy of using forms of rational recreation to monitor and control popular culture has evolved within the framework of social class divisions. In this context, it is believed that sport and leisure help to keep the masses entertained, diverted and committed to an ideology which is largely supportive of the status quo. But the problem of order in Northern Ireland is not primarily rooted in horizontal social divisions. Sectarianism cuts vertically across classes, with the most bitter divisions and antagonisms being manifest between groups of working-class Protestants and Catholics. Clearly, it was the intention of the British Government, through D.E.N.I. and the 26 district councils, to use public sport and leisure provision to help to quell the civil unrest which made the Province virtually ungovernable during the first phase of the Troubles in the late 1960s and early 1970s. It is by no means certain, however, that the introduction of an extensive network of public leisure facilities, particularly in Belfast and Londonderry, helped to get young people off the streets or changed people's attitudes towards political violence. It may be that as an unintended consequence of Westminster's intervention, rather than helping to promote integration, for the most part leisure centres have been adopted by one half of the community at the expense of the other and vice versa, and separate sectarian identities have been sharpened. Thus, in applying a British model of community recreation to Northern Ireland, the state may have done something to undermine the potential for intra-community anti-social behaviour at the expense of feeding the more potent sectarian cross-community divisions which are the source of serious political violence in the Province. There can be little doubt that such provision itself has become a part of the region's complex political equation, as have the activities of the S.C.N.I. and the approach taken to sport and games in Northern Ireland's divided school system. Admirable though the objectives may be, it is highly unlikely that a belated attempt to rectify some of these errors through a vigorous community relations campaign will seriously narrow the distance between the two rival factions.

CONCLUSION

SPORT, POLITICS AND NATIONAL IDENTITY: THE LESSONS OF NORTHERN IRELAND

This study has sought to reveal the extent to which sport and leisure in Northern Ireland are politicised both at the level of formal political structures and that of popular culture. We have also attempted to show how sport and leisure in the Province are, in a variety of ways, intimately bound up with the politics of national and community division. As a consequence of our endeavours to identify and understand the forces which shape and, to some extent, are shaped by the Province's sport and leisure culture, it has been necessary to learn much about the broader structures and processes which frame and sustain Northern Ireland's ongoing political crisis. In this sense, sport in Northern Ireland can best be understood as a two-way mirror which not only reflects transcending social and political conflict, but also, in certain important instances, helps to sustain that conflict. The aim of this concluding chapter is to review our findings in the light of the theory of sport politics and power relations presented in Chapter 1, paying particular attention to the issues of sport and nationalism and sport and the state.

SPORT AND NATIONALISM

While organised physical recreations can be traced back to before the classical period, sport as we know it today is the product of developments which took place in the nineteenth century, largely in western Europe and particularly in Britain. Among a complex interplay of forces which shaped the beginnings of modern sport, was a perceived need to nurture and symbolise a growing sense of nationhood and to project this on to an international stage. As John Wilson observes:

> The years between 1870 and 1914 can be regarded as the period when state, nation and society began to converge. Seen from below, the state increasingly defined the largest stage on which the crucial activities determining human lives as subjects and citizens were played out. Political elites became increasingly aware of the importance of 'irrational' elements, such as national holidays, ceremonies and festivals in binding the loyalty of people to this new entity and for marking the boundaries between 'us' and 'them' – aliens, foreigners, strangers. . . . all manner of leisure pursuits, and sport in particular, have played an important role in these affirmations of identity and unity. (Wilson, 1988: 149)

As we have seen, the emergence of the G.A.A. in Ireland can be understood in these terms. The period in question was one of intensive economic and political competition between major industrial and colonial powers, such as Britain, Germany, France and, increasingly, the United States. The most serious outcome of this international rivalry was the Great War. In addition to global military conflict, however, there was a concomitant struggle for world cultural hegemony within which sport became a major weapon. The Great War did not end nationalism. Rather, it gave competing nation states sharper definition and aided the emergence of other major players in the form of the United States and the Soviet Union. Just as these developments set the pattern for economic, diplomatic and military affiliation and conflict for the remainder of the twentieth century, so too did they set the ground rules for the politicisation of sport in the modern world. Furthermore, because athletic prowess is relatively cheaper to procure than military might, economic development or scientific eminence, the superpower strategy of linking sporting success with national prestige has been seized upon by a range of developing and underdeveloped states such as Cuba, Kenya, and Ethiopia (Filger, 1981: 212). Indeed, in the post-colonial period many newly independent states have utilised sport as one of the major channels for establishing a sense of national identity which might transcend traditional tribal affiliations. Thus, as the twentieth century has progressed, sport has developed as a tool of politics in a truly global sense.

Hoberman (1984) has clearly demonstrated that political ideology is the handmaiden of nationalism and the symbolic power of sport renders it extremely vulnerable to ideological exploitation in the service of a range of sometimes contradictory nationalistic causes. For instance, as we have already seen, soldiers of the Royal Scots Regiment were obliged to withdraw from association football in Ireland in order to take part in the Boer War. Meanwhile, Irish nationalists campaigned against the recruitment of Irishmen to fight in South Africa and, at the symbolic level, sympathetic elements within the G.A.A. baited the British by renaming certain clubs after Boer leaders, such as General De Wet (Corry, 1989: 88). For their part, Unionists in Northern Ireland were happy to follow the example of mainland English patriots in naming a section of the national football stadium the Spion Kop in memory of those British servicemen who lost their lives at this famous battle. In this way, Irish nationalists and British loyalists were able to use both sport and the Boer War to express mutually antagonistic ideological messages.

With all of this in mind, it is too much to hope that sport can regularly act as the harbinger of international goodwill. Indeed, most of the evidence available suggests that the popular belief that sport can act as a peacemaker between rival nations and regional political factions, is an ideal which does not stand up to empirical scrutiny. Political relationships are rarely forged purely through cultural contacts. The notion of 'ping-pong diplomacy' – that is improving foreign relations through international sporting contacts – is only operationally valid when the nations in question are already well on the way towards formalising friendships, such as was the case when the phrase was originally coined to describe the opening of political relations between China and the United States. A considerable amount of political and diplomatic groundwork had to be done before the easing of relations between the two superpowers could be made public through an exchange of visits by national table-tennis teams. Similar efforts to improve relations between Cuba and the United States using sport as a medium have failed precisely because the political gulf between these two nations is so great that it cannot be narrowed by sporting and cultural links, which themselves are difficult to sustain in an atmosphere of mutual mistrust (Sugden *et al.*, 1990). In fact, rather than being a positive diplomatic tool, sport is more often used as an aggressive political lever. The breaking off of sporting relations between nations is usually one of the earliest steps taken on the modern warpath.

In the most extreme circumstances it has been demonstrated that sport can actually kindle existing resentments into open hostility. Despite or perhaps because of its universality, association football, more than any other sport, has facilitated the expression of national and regional loyalties. The legendary 'soccer war' between El Salvador and Honduras demonstrates clearly how sport can serve as a catalyst for serious international conflict. Incidents between rival spectators in 1969 at two World Cup qualifying football matches between these two nations, which were already involved in a long-standing political and economic dispute, sparked off a major military conflict resulting in an estimated 6,000 dead and 24,000 wounded (Strenk, 1979). The second match, which took place in San Salvador, was witnessed by Polish journalist, Ryszard Kapuscinski, and his recollections of the event vividly capture a moment of sporting nationalistic fervour:

> The screaming fans broke all of the windows in the hotel and threw rotten eggs, dead rats and stinking rags inside. The players were taken to the match in armoured cars of the 1st Salvadoran Mechanised Division, which saved them from revenge and bloodshed at the hands of the mob that lined the route, holding up portraits of the national heroine Amelia Bolanios. The army surrounded the ground. On the pitch stood a cordon of soldiers from a crack regiment of the Guardia Nacional, armed with sub-machine guns. During the playing of the Honduran national anthem the crowd roared and whistled. Next, instead of the Honduran flag – which had been burnt before the eyes of the spectators, driving them mad with joy – the hosts ran a dirty, tattered dishrag up the flagpole. (Kapuscinski, 1990)

In fact, football in Central and South America is regularly disrupted by the intervention of regional and national political differences. Likewise, in parts of Africa the quest to overcome tribalism has been set back by the excessive partisanship of football supporters (Monnington, 1986: 159). In view of the persistent potential for conflict in the Middle East and in order to avoid further aggravating Israeli/Arab relations, for the purposes of World Cup qualification, F.I.F.A. first arranged for Israel to compete in a European section. This led to protests from the Soviet Union and other eastern European nations, and F.I.F.A.'s response was to relocate Israel in the Pacific qualifying zone.

If we turn our attention to Europe, it can be seen that at a time when the European Community is doing its best to break down those traditional notions of separate identity and nationhood which have helped to precipitate two world wars and led to numerous regional conflicts, sport in general and football in particular continue to provide avenues for popular, nationalistic and ethnocentric expression. We have already touched upon the regional rivalries which are integral to football violence in England. Similarly, but to an even greater extent, in Spain the antipathy between Basques, Catalans and Castilians finds public expression in the Spanish football league in much the same way as long-standing rivalries between the former city states which now make up Italy find a public forum through that country's professional football programme. Encounters between Germany and Holland in recent memory have been conducted in a hostile atmosphere which cannot be understood in terms of contemporary political and economic relations between the two countries, but only by reference to older rivalries and above all to the events of the Second World War. If it seems strange that a sports event can evoke memories of battles fought 50 years earlier, the rivalry between England and Scotland is more peculiar still. Even though they have been part of the same political unit for almost 300 years, the antipathy between the two countries remains strong. There were few fixtures more keenly contested among players and supporters than the annual soccer match between them and it was not unusual to see Scottish supporters waving banners reminding their opponents of Scotland's military victory over the English at the Battle of Bannockburn, fought in 1314! In general terms, international soccer competitions, such as the European Championships and the World Cup, are stages not only for footballing skill, but also for gross displays of nationalism which often spill over into violent confrontations between rival groups of supporters.

Damaging xenophobic associations with sport are by no means restricted to soccer however and, despite the multilateralist proclamations of governments and governing bodies, sport in general is still a powerful cultural metaphor for regional and international aggression. Much as they may have been resurrected in the name of international goodwill and global understanding, as the greatest and most watched show on earth, the modern Olympics have been so crippled by the burdens of nationalism that their future has been seriously questioned. Many aspects of this nationalism are introduced by outside agencies. However, as we have seen in the case of hockey in Northern Ireland, the Olympic movement is itself highly committed to the concept of national representation. So long as agreements on the flying of national flags and the playing of national anthems remain as prerequisites to Olympic participation, in an epoch of ethnic and national conflict the Olympics will continue to be one of the world's greatest political showcases.

Thus, wherever there are national or regional conflicts between societies which share a passion for sports, those conflicts will be reflected in and carried on through respective sporting cultures, and Northern Ireland is not an exception to this general rule. However, such statements are made against a background in which many administrators of sport and leisure in Ireland continue to claim that their sphere of influence is essentially apolitical, some going so far as to suggest that sport can even be used as a means to integrate the rival communities instead of separating them. In the light of our overall analysis, it would appear that such claims are located in the realm of hope rather than grounded in reality. The optimism which drives those who are involved in the various sport-based community relations projects in Northern Ireland is commendable and, as we have observed, can be well founded in the case of carefully controlled situations involving small numbers of people. Overall, however, the foregoing analysis leads to the more pessimistic conclusion that sport and leisure in Northern Ireland are deeply implicated in the politics of sectarian division.

It is unimaginable that Gaelic sport could ever become widely popular within the Protestant community. Indeed, there is absolutely no reason why it should, given the G.A.A.'s pivotal role as a celebrant of things Irish and as a major antagonist towards that British way of life to which Ulster Protestants feel and claim allegiance. The irony of the G.A.A. remaining one of the last defenders of nineteenth-century English sporting ideals makes no material difference.

Rugby union and the other sports which remain organically linked to the British presence in Ireland play a curiously double-headed role today. On the one hand, these sports have shown themselves capable of bringing together Catholics and Protestants from the two parts of Ireland. On the other, they have done little or nothing to reconcile the two communities in Northern Ireland where the sports are recognised as Protestant, regardless of the existence of all-Ireland sides and cross-border leagues and competitions. Furthermore, given the middle-class character of most, if not all, of these sports, any integrative potential which they might possess would relate only to those people who, for the most part, stay aloof from the Troubles and not to members of the rival working-class communities who have produced the majority of those who perpetrate political violence and have suffered most in the course of the crisis.

Other sports which developed in Ireland as a result of the British presence have now become so universally popular that it is impossible for the Protestant community to claim them for themselves. Notable among these is association football. Its popularity and global appeal might suggest that football has a far greater capacity than other sports to bring together people of different races, classes, religious and ethnic affiliations. However, the preceding analysis clearly shows that the game's popularity has, in many ways, been its greatest downfall. The high emotional attachment which soccer generates, and the feelings of collective identity and group solidarity which it is capable of generating, has rendered the game extremely vulnerable to exploitation by hooligans, types of nationalists and alliances of the two. Not surprisingly, the development of football in Northern Ireland has conformed to the general pattern. Although the game integrates in the sense of bringing Catholics and Protestants together, the very fact that it is played and watched by members of both communities means that association football, unlike other major sports in the Province, affords regular opportunities for displays of sectarian feelings which can often result in violence. In addition, since football is a characteristically working-class pastime in Northern Ireland, the antagonists in these confrontations are predominantly members of communities which are most intimately involved at the cutting-edge of the Troubles.

By progressively increasing its involvement in and control over sport and leisure in Northern Ireland, the British state has tacitly acknowledged the importance of this area of popular culture in the politics of division. In this regard, how are we to assess the contribution of the state to the Province's sport and leisure infrastructure?

SPORT, LEISURE AND THE STATE IN NORTHERN IRELAND

Although the state is commonly regarded as the most important and most genuinely universal human association in the modern world, there is little agreement as to its precise nature and functions. Is it a neutral body concerned with the dispassionate arbitration of needs and allocation of resources among individuals? Is it a broker between the various social classes and interest groups within its jurisdiction? Or is it the agency which ultimately acts in the interests of a dominant social formation, and if so, what is the precise nature of the relationship between state and ruling elite? Despite the complexity of these questions a broad distinction has been made between pluralist (liberal democratic/functionalist) and Marxist theories of the state, but even within these traditions, rival analyses abound. As Gruneau (1982) has demonstrated, the theoretical confusion surrounding the nature of the state is replicated within the literature concerned with the relationship between sport and political institutions.

The debate between pluralists and Marxists has largely been centred on the relative importance of force *vis-à-vis* consent in the political process. According to the classical Marxist view, the state was defined as 'a committee for managing the common affairs of the whole bourgeoise' (Marx and Engels, 1848, in 1967 edition: 82). In other words, it is an instrument which is used by an economically dominant class to further its own class interests and at the same time arrest the potential for class conflict.

For pluralists, on the other hand, the state represents a value-free mechanism through which society seeks to satisfy conflicting interests and maintain consensus. In the past these images of the state have tended to be mutually exclusive. However, although emanating from the Marxist tradition, the political analysis of Antonio Gramsci explains that, in advanced capitalist society, political power is the result of the fusion of force and consent, conceptualised by him in an expanded theory of the state in which political and civil society are distinguished. Political society consists of those agencies which formally represent constitutional authority and which for many pluralists and Marxists alone constitute a state: the executive, the judiciary and the forces of law and order. Civil society, according to Gramsci, is made up of a range of semi-autonomous institutions and activities, such as education, the church, the media, sport, leisure and other areas of popular culture. Gramsci assigns to the latter cultural institutions a discrete political role, but as Hoare and Nowell Smith (Gramsci, 1971) point out in their editorial commentary on his *Prison Notebooks*, the distinction between political and civil society is frequently blurred. This reflects the complex relationship between the two realms which operates in practice, particularly during times of civil strife. Taking education as one example, there is an obvious tension within a system which is subject to control at both a central and local level. Furthermore, education interpreted in its broadest possible sense of inculcating certain *mores*, values and beliefs within the population, is central to the aims of many government bodies, including those associated with sport and leisure. Nevertheless, the conceptual distinction between political and civil society, as Perry Anderson has argued, is valuable as a 'practico-indicative concept' through which 'an indispensable line of demarcation within the politico-ideological superstructures of capitalism can be established' (Anderson, 1976: 35). It is as a metaphor for the dialectical relationship between force and consent in liberal democracies that this distinction is best employed for analytical purposes.

Gramsci's civil society is the terrain on which those responsible for the articulation and dissemination of ideas in a variety of ways, attempt to attract the mass of the population and influence them towards certain values and aspirations. Although some of the functionaries of civil society are antagonistic to the dominant group and purvey oppositional attitudes to their public, in normal circumstances the majority act in such a way as to provide widespread acceptance by the population of the world view expressed by those in positions of political power. The result is the cultural, ideological and moral authority of the ruling class, which Gramsci refers to as hegemony. Hegemonic rule can be said to exist when the vast majority of citizens give their consent, either actively or passively, to the existing social order. At no time is this a static condition inasmuch as counter-hegemonic challenges continue to be made and the ruling elite is constantly obliged to renegotiate the conditions under which its ideology remains dominant. Furthermore, Gramsci did not believe that coercion ever ceases to be an element in the maintenance of political order in western societies. Thus, in times of political crisis, when hegemonic rule is threatened, not only does the dominant group become increasingly interventionist in the affairs of civil society, but through the mechanisms of political society, it has recourse to open displays of coercive power.

Gramsci's thesis was originally developed to explain the failure of class-based revolutionary politics in his own native Italy and elsewhere in western Europe in the first quarter of the twentieth century. However, as someone who had begun his political life as a Sardinian nationalist and who frequently confronted the question of national popular culture in his prison writings, he was conscious of the existence of categories of social stratification other than class. Partly because of his own commitment to Marxist discourse, but equally because of the narrow concerns of other Marxist scholars who have used his work, Gramsci's embryonic awareness of vertical social divisions remained undeveloped in his own work and unexplored by many of his more fervent admirers. As we shall see, when used flexibly, Gramscian concepts have considerable explanatory power when applied to societies such as Northern Ireland wherein horizontal divisions of social class are cross-cut by more powerful vertical divisions of national, ethnic and cultural origin.

Perhaps the most sophisticated application of Gramsci's theoretical framework to the world of sport can be found in the work of John Hargreaves (1986). The main thrust of his analysis is directed towards revealing the multifaceted ways through which sport has been implicated in the achievement, maintenance and development of bourgeois hegemony in British society during the last century and a half. This, he argues, has been achieved through two related processes: the role of sport in the fragmentation of the working class in particular and subordinate groups in general; and their reconstitution 'within a unified social formation, under bourgeois hegemony' (ibid.: 209). Hargreaves goes to great lengths to show how complex these processes are and is especially careful to point out that there has been no single, all powerful agency involved in the instrumental manipulation of sports. Nevertheless, he argues that the state, or political society in Gramscian terminology, has had a pivotal role in the coordination of a variety of institutional programmes which have sought to intervene in areas of popular culture which either pose a threat to the status quo or are seen to have particular utility in strengthening the hegemonic rule of the dominant group in society.   *the state*

Almost by definition, in societies where political society and civil society complement each other in such a way as to secure a basis for the exercise of political power – that is, when hegemony is established – the instrumental intervention of the state into the realm of popular culture is difficult to discern. As Hargreaves observes, it is during periods when the established order is threatened that the state is forced to reveal its hand in an attempt to re-establish hegemonic domination. He refers to these periods as 'turning points in the relationships between sports and the power network' (ibid.: 208). One such turning point occurred during the first half of the nineteenth century as an ascendant bourgeois class assumed political control and used its power to discipline the free time of those subordinate groups in society which were to constitute the industrial working class. Popular recreations and sports were both the target and the instrument of reformist strategies and this established a pattern which has remained more or less intact right up to the latter part of the twentieth century.

While there has been no wholesale challenge to the established order, at various times the position of the ruling class has had to be strengthened by a variety of state-sponsored initiatives, including interventions into the world of sport. For instance, in response to a 'moral panic' over the anti-social aspects of youth culture in the post-Second World War period, the British Government launched a range of sport-related programmes in an attempt to re-establish the ethical and cultural authority of the defenders of the established order (ibid.: 183). However, despite the worst fears of respectable citizens, the activities of Teddy Boys, Mods, Rockers, Hippies, Skinheads and Punks never seriously constituted a threat to the fabric of British society. With reflection, the same can be said of the series of inner-city riots which took place in the 1980s in areas such as Brixton, St Pauls, Toxteth and Broadwater Farm. These represented fleeting moments of challenge to the established order rather than turning points in power relations. Significantly, however, in the wake of the inner-city riots, there was a noticeable, albeit temporary, increase in public sport and leisure provision in the worst affected areas. Nevertheless, in Britain in general, it has been possible to keep state intervention in sport and other areas of popular culture to a minimum to the extent that, when such interventions do occur, they can be easily passed off as little more than the response of government to genuine community needs in the areas of health and social welfare.

Although there has been no sustained threat to political stability in Britain during the twentieth century, this is hardly the case in Northern Ireland, where there has been a real and potent challenge to the rule of the British Government since the original partition of Ireland in 1921, and in particular in the period since 1969. After partition Northern Ireland was ruled by a devolved government under the sovereignty of British jurisdiction. This political arrangement was acceptable to the unionist section of the population which regarded itself as primarily British. However, the fit between political and civil society disregarded the existence within Northern Ireland of a separate and distinctive cultural network which can be said to constitute a Catholic-Irish civil society. In 1972 the devolved government at Stormont was prorogued and direct rule from Westminster was introduced. In the absence of significant local involvement in the composition and operation of political society, the link between unionist civil society and the state has been weakened. Thus, the situation in Northern Ireland can now be characterised as one of hegemonic crisis created by the failure of political society adequately to complement either of the civil societies, which between them encompass the vast majority of the citizens whose consent is necessary for the establishment of political order. Not only has this necessitated far greater recourse to the use of coercive power in Northern

Ireland than in other parts of the United Kingdom, but it has also required a much higher level of direct state intervention into popular culture.

What then in general can be learned from the Northern Ireland experience? The most obvious point is that as aspects of civil society, sport and leisure only reveal themselves clearly as foci for political/hegemonic struggle during times of protracted civil unrest. Such manifestations may well be the end results of continuous historical processes, but it is only when the cooperation and control of civil society itself is at stake, as in Northern Ireland, that the state is forced to show its hand. However, what the state has learned to its cost in the Province is that as elements of civil society, neither sport nor leisure can be mobilised automatically in support of the established forces of law and order. They are both vital elements of popular culture and, as such, are likely to be part and parcel of the undercurrents which fuel dissent. For this reason, they are neither easy to penetrate nor manipulate and, to paraphrase Ralph Miliband's argument, once the state targets sport and leisure as battle fronts in the war to establish hegemony it discovers them to be 'highly contested territory' (Miliband, 1977: 51–4).

The picture is further complicated by the fact that civil society in Northern Ireland is terrain highly contested not just between social classes, but also between Catholics and Protestants, various groupings of Nationalists and Loyalists, and the different agencies of the British state. In terms of sport and leisure, the state in Northern Ireland has at least two faces. One is an open and smiling countenance which supports community integration and cross-border cooperation, while at the same time, closer to the scene, there is a stiff upper-lip which accompanies coercion and force to maintain the status quo. Accordingly, on the surface a conventional British model of community recreation and sport for all is encouraged. In practice, however, this model tends to reinforce rather than ameliorate sectarian divisions and at a local level, through the activities of politically motivated pressure groups, local politicians and ultimately the security forces, sport and leisure have become part of Northern Ireland's wider political conflict. Thus, while sport and leisure may not represent the Province's most important battleground, by no means are they politically insignificant.

By applying Gramscian concepts to Northern Ireland we have tried to show that the conceptual distinction between political and civil society can be usefully applied to the provision of sport and leisure so long as the application is flexible enough to accommodate fragmentation within the state while at the same time allowing for the existence of significant counter-hegemonic social formations within society outside of social classes. Indeed, one of the main problems with using Gramsci in the analysis of contemporary political and social processes is that hitherto many Marxist scholars who have used his model have focused almost exclusively on class to the exclusion of other obviously important status groupings such as nationalism, ethnicity, race, gender and sectarianism. Any theoretical framework which does not account for the latter can have little explanatory power in Northern Ireland.

It seems that there is no aspect of modern, mass society, other than war or rumour of war, which does more than sport to arouse nationalism, racism, ethnocentrism and sectarianism. It may help to strengthen affection between friends, even build bridges between those who see mutual advantage in establishing lines of communication and trade, but between enemies, sport reinforces the basis of enmity and creates new sources of antagonism. Furthermore, we believe that because of its deeply social nature and its flexible capacity to mobilise popular sentiment, the culture surrounding sport is often terrain contested between competing elements of civil society and of the politically constituted state. Consequently, as the state has assumed enlarged significance in the twentieth century, sport and affiliated activities have become increasingly politicised.

We have argued that not only is it difficult for sports participants in Northern Ireland to extricate themselves from the close linkage of sport and politics, but also that many do not wish to see any integration of sport beyond that which already exists. Indeed, in some areas, notably association football, added spice is given to the structure of competition as a direct result of sectarian dimensions. In the case of Gaelic sports, the celebration of Irish national cultural exclusiveness is vital to their continued appeal in Northern Ireland. Generally, cultural division is a way of life in Northern Ireland to such a degree that most of the population derive comfort from the totems of their separate civil societies. Thus, the state in Northern Ireland is faced with a dilemma. It has an ideological commitment to and statutory responsibility for encouraging and facilitating widespread participation in sport and leisure. However, in fulfilling this commitment it actually provides added scope for sectarian differentiation. As a result, the state in its traditional coercive guise finds itself policing those divisive areas of popular culture which, in its welfarist role, it helps to sustain.

This dilemma between force and consent cannot be resolved within the confines of sport and leisure. Any resolution to Northern Ireland's political crisis must be based upon the widest possible range of economic, political and cultural institutions. By virtue of their central location in the rival civil societies, sport and leisure would have a role to play in such a scenario. However, it is pointless to tamper with sport alone when other related elements of civil society, such as the school system, continue to foster a form of cultural apartheid. In the meantime, while the various elements of the state agonise over the place of sport in a divided society, at a grass-roots level the games themselves continue to thrive, despite and, in some instances, because of their sectarian complexions. Like the boy who can bring a game to an end when his team is losing simply because he owns the ball, many sports people in Northern Ireland are comforted by the belief that, at least for the time being, the ball, whatever its shape, belongs to them and decisions about who can play with it are ultimately theirs.

REFERENCES

Anderson, P., 1976, The antinomies of Antonio Gramsci, *New Left Review*, 100: 5–78

Bailey, P., 1989, Leisure, culture and the historian: reviewing the first generation of leisure historiography in Britain, *Leisure Studies*, 8 (2): 67–127

Belfast News Letter, Belfast, various dates

Belfast Telegraph, Belfast, various dates

Bergin, S. and Scott, D., 1980, Cricket in Ireland, in E.W. Swanton (ed.), *Barclays World of Cricket*, Collins, London: 508–510

Berki, R.N., 1977, *The History of Political Thought. A Short Introduction*, Dent, London

Brodie, M., 1980, *One Hundred Years of Irish Football*, Blackstaff, Belfast

Brohm, J.-M., 1978, *Sport: A Prison of Measured Time*, Ink Links, London

Browning, R., 1955, *A History of Golf. The Royal and Ancient Game*, Dent, London

Central Council for Physical Recreation, 1991, *The Organisation of Sport and Recreation in Britain*, CCPR, London

Clarke, J. and Critcher, C., 1985, *The Devil Makes Work. Leisure in Capitalist Britain*, Macmillan, Basingstoke

Clarke, J., Hall, S., Jefferson, T. and Roberts, B., 1976, Subcultures, cultures and class in S. Hall and T. Jefferson (eds), *Resistance Through Rituals. Youth Subcultures in Post-war Britain*, Hutchinson, London: 9–79

Cliftonville Cricket Club, 1990, *Souvenir Brochure*

Corry, E., 1989, *Catch and Kick*, Poolbeg, Dublin

Crozier, M. (ed.), 1990, *Cultural Traditions in Northern Ireland. Proceedings of the Cultural Traditions Group Conference*, Institute of Irish Studies, Queen's University, Belfast

Cunningham, H., 1980, *Leisure in the Industrial Revolution c1780–c1880*, Croom Helm, London

Dagg, T.S.C., 1944, *Hockey in Ireland*, The Kerryman Limited, Tralee

Dahl, R.A., 1976, *Modern Political Analysis*, Prentice-Hall Inc., Englewood Cliffs, New Jersey de Búrca, M., 1980, *The GAA. A History*, Cumann Lúthchleas Gael, Dublin

de Búrca, M., 1990, *Michael Cusack and the GAA*, Anvil, Dublin

Department of the Environment, 1989, *Value for Money Study: Leisure Facilities*, HMSO

Diffley, S., 1973, *The Men in Green: The Story of Irish Rugby*, Pelham Books, London

Elias, N. and Dunning, E., 1986, *The Quest for Excitement*, Blackwell, Oxford

Filger, S.K., 1981, *Sport and Play in American Life*, Saunders, Philadelphia

Frazer, D.I., 1990, An analysis of sectarianism and sports participation in Dungannon district. Unpublished MA dissertation, University of Ulster

Gaelic Athletic Association Rules, 1991, GAA, Croke Park, Dublin

Gibson, W.H., 1988, *Early Irish Golf. The First Courses, Clubs and Pioneers*, Oakleaf, Nass, Co. Kildare

Gramsci, A., 1971, *Selections from the Prison Notebooks*, in Q. Hoare and G. Nowell Smith (eds), Lawrence and Wishart, London

Griffin, P., 1990, *The Politics of Irish Athletics, 1850–1990*, Marathon Publications, Ballinamore, Co. Leitrim

Gruneau, R., 1982, Sport and the debate on the state, in H. Cantelon and R. Gruneau (eds), *Sport, Culture and the Modern State*, University of Toronto Press, Toronto: 1–38

Guardian, Manchester, various dates

Hall, S., 1986, Popular culture and the state, in T. Bennett, C. Mercer and J. Woollacott (eds), *Popular Culture and Social Relations*, Open University Press, Milton Keynes: 22–49

Hargreaves, J., 1986, *Sport and Popular Culture: A Social and Historical Analysis of Popular Sports in Britain*, Polity Press, Cambridge

Haywood, L., 1986, Hegemony – another blind alley for the study of sport, in J.A. Mangan and R.B. Small (eds), *Sport, Culture, Society. International, Historical and Sociological Perspectives*, E. and F.N. Spon, London: 234–239

Hebdige, D., 1979, *Subculture. The Meaning of Style*, Methuen, London

Hoberman, J., 1984, *Sport and Political Ideology*, Heinemann, London

Hoberman, J., 1992, Sport and political ideology in the post-communist age. Presented at 'The changing politics of sport conference', Warwick University

Hoch, P., 1972, *Rip off the Big Game*, Anchor Books, Garden City, New York

Holt, R., 1989, *Sport and the British. A Modern History*, Clarendon Press, Oxford

Hone, W.P., 1956, *Cricket in Ireland*, The Kerryman Limited, Tralee

Huntley, D., 1988, An analysis of leisure centre provision in Belfast. Unpublished BA dissertation, University of Ulster

Irish News, Belfast, various dates

Irish Times, Dublin, various dates

Kapuscinski, R., 1990, *Soccer War*, Granta Books, London

Kennedy, J., 1989, *Belfast Celtic*, Pretani Press, Belfast

Knox, C., 1989, Local government leisure services: planning and politics in Northern Ireland. Unpublished D Phil thesis, University of Ulster

Langhammer, M., 1989, Irish rugby: towards professionalisation, *A Belfast Magazine*, 3 (5): 12–15

McCarthy, J., 1892, Ireland, in Rev. Frank Marshall (ed.), *Football. The Rugby Union Game*, cited in E. Van Esbeck, 1974, *One Hundred Years of Irish Rugby*, Gill and Macmillan, Dublin

McGivern, N.P., 1991, Examination of patterns of association football support as a way of determining national identity in Northern Ireland. Unpublished BA dissertation, University of Ulster

Malcolmson, R.W., 1973, *Popular Recreations in English Society 1700–1850*, Cambridge University Press, Cambridge

Mandle, W.F., 1987, *The Gaelic Athletic Association and Irish Nationalist Politics, 1884–1924*, Christopher Helm/Gill and Macmillan, London and Dublin

Marx, K. and Engels, F., 1967, *The Communist Manifesto*, Penguin, Harmondsworth

Miliband, R., 1977, *Marxism and Politics*, Oxford University Press, Oxford

Miller, D.W., 1978, *Queen's Rebels. Ulster Loyalism in Historical Perspective*, Gill and Macmillan, Dublin

Monnington, T., 1986, The politics of black African sport, in L. Allison (ed.), *The Politics of Sport*, Manchester University Press, Manchester: 149–73

Murray, D., 1985, *Worlds Apart. Segregated Schools in Northern Ireland*, Appletree Press, Belfast

Nairn, T., 1981, *The Break-up of Britain* (revised edn), Verso, London

Northern Ireland Council for Educational Development, 1988, *Education for Mutual Understanding. A Guide*, NICED

Northern Ireland Information Service

O'Dowd, L., Rolston, B. and Tomlinson, M., 1980, *Northern Ireland. Between Civil Rights and Civil War*, CSE Books, London

O Muilleoir, M., 1989, Sinn Fein Press Release, No. 230261

Platt, W.H.W., 1986, *A History of Derry City Football and Athletic Club, 1929–1972*, Author, Coleraine

Puirseal, P., 1982, *The GAA in its Time*, Purcell, Dublin

Roberts, K., 1983, *Leisure and Youth*, Allen and Unwin, London

Roberts, K., 1989, *Community Response to Sports Centre Provision in Belfast*, Belfast City Council, Belfast

Scotland on Sunday, Edinburgh

Sports Council (Northern Ireland). Annual reports, Belfast, various dates

Sports Illustrated, New York

Spotlight, BBC Television (Northern Ireland), various dates

Stewart, A.T.Q., 1977, *The Narrow Ground*, Faber and Faber, London

Strenk, A., 1979, Sport as an international and diplomatic tool, in A. Yiannakis, T.D. McIntyre, M.J. Melnick and D.P. Hart (eds), *Sport Sociology. Contemporary Themes*, 3rd edition, Kendal Hunt, Dubuque: 71–74

Sugden, J., 1991, Belfast united: encouraging cross-community relations through sport in Northern Ireland, *Journal of Sport and Social Issues*, 15 (1): 59–80

Sugden J. and Bairner, A., 1986, Northern Ireland: sport in a divided society, in L. Allison (ed.), *The Politics of Sport*, Manchester University Press, Manchester: 90–117

Sugden, J., Tomlinson, A. and McCartan, E., 1990, The making and remaking of white lightening in Cuba: politics, sport and physical education 30 years after the revolution, *Arena Review*, 14 (1): 101–109

Sugden, J. and Yiannakis, A., 1987 (3rd edn), Sport and juvenile delinquency: a theoretical base, in A. Yiannakis, T.D. McIntyre, M.J. Melnick and D.P. Hart (eds), *Sport Sociology. Contemporary Themes*, 3rd edition, Kendal Hunt, Dubuque: 115–118

Sunday Life, Belfast, various dates

Sunday Times, London, various dates

Sunday Tribune, Dublin, various dates

Ulster News Letter, Belfast, various dates

Van Esbeck, E., 1974, *One Hundred Years of Irish Rugby*, Gill and Macmillan, Dublin

Van Esbeck, E., 1986, *The Story of Irish Rugby*, Stanley Paul, London

West, T., 1991, *The Bold Collegians. The Development of Sport in Trinity College, Dublin*, The Lilliput Press, Dublin

Williams, G., 1989, Rugby union, in T. Mason (ed.), *Sport in Britain. A Social History*, Cambridge University Press, Cambridge

Wilson, J., 1988, *Politics and Leisure*, Unwin Hyman, Boston

INDEX